Government
IN THE DIGITAL AGE

Government
IN THE DIGITAL AGE

PAUL GOSLING

Sponsored by

BOWERDEAN
Publishing Company Limited

Work in the Digital Age

A new series of books explaining how the 'new technology' – the Internet, CD-ROM, on-line services, virtual reality etc. – will have an impact on work of different kinds. Titles already published include *Financial Services in the Digital Age* by Paul Gosling, *Retail in the Digital Age* by Nigel Cope and *Travel in the Digital Age* by Linsey McNeil. Also planned are titles on education and publishing.

Acknowledgements

This book would not have been possible without the enormous assistance given by many people. ICL has not only sponsored the book, but provided valuable advice, and made available senior managers to explain the corporation's involvement with a range of developments.

I would particularly like to thank John Cheetham, Graham Goulden, Dave Denison, John Elmore, George Hall and Richard Stokes at ICL for their valuable help and encouragement.

The European Commission and its various directorates have been extremely helpful, and very generous with their documents and e-mails. EDS were both hospitable and supportive in helping me with my research. Thanks, too, to all the too numerous to mention organisations that have provided me, free of charge, with research papers and other publications. But particular thanks go to Alan Burkitt-Gray, editor of the magazine *Electronic Government International*, for providing back copies which have proved invaluable.

I am particularly grateful to Neil Barrett and Bull Information Systems for their assistance, and to Neil for supplying me with copies of various papers, and for talking over with me some of the ideas in the book and reading through the manuscript. I am indebted to Simon Wallace for his valued help with chapter five.

Most of all thanks go to Robert Dudley, the publisher, and David Bowen, the series editor, for their confidence and support.

Any errors are entirely the author's responsibility.

Published by The Bowerdean Publishing Company Ltd.
of 8 Abbotstone Road, London SW15 1QR

First published in 1997

Paul Gosling has asserted his right under the Copyright, Designs and Patents Act, 1988, to be identified as Author of this Work.

All rights reserved.

No part of this publication may be reproduced, stored in a retrieval system or transmitted in any form or by any means, electronic, mechanical, photocopying, recording or otherwise except brief extracts for the purpose of review, without prior written permission of the publishers.

Any paperback edition of this book whether published simultaneously with or subsequent to the casebound edition is sold subject to the condition that it shall not, by way of trade, be lent, resold, hired out or otherwise disposed of without the publisher's consent, in any form of binding or cover other than that in which it was published.

British Library Cataloguing-in-Publication Data.
A catalogue record for this book is available from the British Library.

ISBN 0 906097 84 3

Designed by the Senate
Printed by Wessex Press Group Ltd

CONTENTS

	Glossary	8
CHAPTER 1	Introduction	10
CHAPTER 2	Electronic democracy	16
CHAPTER 3	The legal system	31
CHAPTER 4	Transport	43
CHAPTER 5	Health	52
CHAPTER 6	The welfare state	64
CHAPTER 7	Learning	77
CHAPTER 8	Information	87
CHAPTER 9	Paying the piper	98
CHAPTER 10	Managing government	108
CHAPTER 11	Government as regulator	126
CHAPTER 12	The future of government	144
CHAPTER 13	Bibliography	153
	Index	156

GLOSSARY

ATM – asynchronous transfer mode – (not to be confused with automated teller machines, which are banks' cash machines) is the latest high speed, high quality telecommunications cabling that allows for tremendously high amounts of data to be communicated at exceedingly high speed.

CITU – Central Information Technology Unit, the Government's think-tank examining possible uses of new technology, attached to the Cabinet Office.

Digital technology converts information into binary code – current on is one, current off is zero.

Electronic purses are the new form of 'plastic money' using smart card technology. They look like a credit or debit card, but have a microprocessor on the back instead of a magnetic strip. They are already being used in parts of the world as a replacement for cash, and the latest generation of personal and network computers contain smart card readers allowing electronic commerce to be conducted on-line, with payment deducted instantly.

ICT is the shorthand for the integrated 'information and communication technology'. This is the development of 'information technology', by connecting computers to one another, and the phrase ICT is generally used in this book in preference to the now rather outdated term IT.

Intelligent agents are pieces of software that search the World Wide Web, sifting through irrelevant information to find the precise information you are looking for.

Internet (the Net) is the informal global electronic information network that electronic mail passes through, and which contains the World Wide Web.

Intranet is a formal electronic information network that is tightly controlled, operating within an organisation, or group of organisations. These might be Local Area Networks (LANs) if they are in one place, or a Wide Area Network (WAN) if in a diversity of sites.

GLOSSARY

Kiosks are interactive terminals, usually sited in public places or stores. A kiosk might give the user journey times and routes for rail connections, and then sell the ticket for the journey.

Multimedia brings together a mix of different media, such as video film, sound, keyboard, touch-screen control, text and video-conferencing. Multimedia units are likely to play an important part in our future work, home and shopping lives.

Network computers (NCs) are predicted to replace personal computers (PCs) within a few years, particularly within the workplace. They are computer terminals, with screens and keyboards, but with little or no hard disk memory, and are consequently much cheaper than PCs. Information is stored in central databases on host computers, part of the same LAN or WAN, and files can be accessed provided the user has security clearance, which can be confirmed either through the use of code words or smart cards.

Outsourcing is a modern management term for the contracting out of non-core functions. Large corporations commonly outsource their information and communication technology (ICT) functions.

Smart cards are pieces of plastic that look like credit cards, but are actually mini-computers.

Telematics is a word sometimes used to describe the converged information and communication technologies.

Video-conferencing combines a telephone conversation with a live video image of the other party. Discussions can be one-to-one, or bring together dozens of participants from around the world. Future multimedia units are likely to incorporate video-conferencing, and many kiosks already do.

World Wide Web is the main message board on the Internet. There are now millions of pages of information on 'the Web', many of which are boring advertisements. Other entries are important pages of unique research. The problem for users is finding the second without wasting time on the first.

❶ Introduction

2008

Today is special – it is general election day. Phil has decided how he is going to vote. He will support the Reform Party because he thinks the other lot have had their day. How absurd it is, Phil tells himself, that he and his family have to go out and vote when they could far more easily do it from home, using their interactive TV.

Debate about whether people should be allowed to vote at home is one of the hottest arguments of the election, and it has encouraged Phil to vote Reform. His father, on the other hand, likes the ritual of going out to vote, and has never stopped grumbling that he can't put his cross on a slip of paper "just like I did for 50 years". They are bound to have a row about it when Phil takes his father to vote.

The Government says it would be wrong to allow people to vote from home electronically, because not everybody has an interactive TV (but almost everybody has). The TV of today is far more than just a device to receive TV programmes. With the advent of digital TV it can receive hundreds of different stations, some dedicated to entertainment, others to home shopping. The TV is also a personal computer, with access to public information services, a video-conference unit, a telephone, as well as allowing users to surf the World Wide Web.

Access to the TV is controlled through smart cards, which contain personal information details, including an image of the holder's iris and a fingerprint, ensuring that only the proper holder of a card can use it. The card is, like the TV, multi-purpose – it is a person's identification, passport, health insurance certificate (accepted throughout the world), driving licence and electronic purse. Of course, it also contains

INTRODUCTION

the person's age, to prevent children accessing unsuitable programmes.

It would be easy to allow people to vote from home, but the five per cent of people without a modern TV would have to go to a public kiosk to vote, and that, says the Government, would be unfair. So — as Phil grumbles to himself — they all have to go out to a kiosk to vote. The result is that far fewer people vote, but the hair shirt mentality wins out, thinks Phil.

At least Phil's father, John, will be able to draw his pension at the same time. The kiosks that they vote at will be activated through their smart cards, but are owned and run by the banks. At a single trip to one of these kiosks — looking like an advanced version of an old-style cash machine — you can buy almost anything from a mortgage to a can of tomatoes. You can move money between your bank accounts, claim your pension and load it onto your smart card; you can look at recent decisions taken by government or your local council, or vote.

Voting is now fully electronic. You stand in front of a kiosk, making sure the camera above you can see you properly, put your index finger on a pad in front of the terminal, and push your smart card into the slot on the side. If the machine is satisfied that the picture of you, the image of your iris, and your fingerprint all match the details shown on your smart card, you are allowed to vote.

The screen shows who your candidates are, which parties they represent, and asks if you know who you want to vote for. If you say 'yes', it displays each candidate in turn, allowing you to list your favourites in order of preference, as is required under the new system of proportional representation. If you say 'no', you can ask for more details on each candidate — asking each the questions you want answered, and back will come replies based on candidates' previously declared statements.

Within minutes of the close of the election the result will be known — despite the complications of proportional representation — through the advanced computer monitoring and calculation of votes.

And within minutes of the results being declared there will be dozens of pressure groups sending e-mail correspondence to their supporters at home asking them to send a copy of the e-mail —with personalised amendments — to the new government, and to the new Members of Parliament. Each elected MP can expect to receive thousands of

GOVERNMENT IN THE DIGITAL AGE

pieces of e-mail by the following day asking them what they intend to do about such issues as a proposed new power station, or a change in food regulation.

More than anything else, the year 2008 really is the age of lobbying.

▲ ▲ ▲

WILL IT REALLY BE LIKE THIS?

WHETHER people will be allowed to vote from home, or whether they will vote from a kiosk is a choice for the politicians – and it will be another political decision whether those kiosks are owned and run by the public sector, or whether they 'piggy-back' the kiosks owned by banks, supermarkets and others in the private sector. But few experts doubt that we will be voting electronically, one way or another, within a few years.

Indeed, some countries have already taken faster steps towards electronic democracy than Britain has. If Britain were less of an insular nation we might recognise that we are at risk of being left behind, not just in the matter of electronic democracy, but in a wide range of applications of digital technology.

However much we might applaud the Conservative government's programmes, such as the 'Government.Direct' green paper and the 'Information Society Initiative', we must recognise that Britain's public services have responded more slowly than some other nations to the changes brought about by the information and communications technology industry (ICT) revolution.

When the Industrial Revolution hit the world in the middle of the 18th century, it had far reaching effects on the distribution of wealth. Entrepreneurs who built the new mills and used the new textile machinery made their fortunes quickly. Families who had made

INTRODUCTION

clothing by hand in their homes were forced into the factories, where they had to work longer hours for less money.

Across the world, countries, too, made and lost their fortunes. Britain had already grown rich, on the back of the triangular trades of slave, cotton and sugar. When those cotton imports were put together with the Industrial Revolution, Britain's place in the world league rose dramatically at the expense of traditional competitors France and Germany.

Today Britain is a country of declining relative importance. It is in the second rank of the hierarchy of the ICT revolution, behind not just the United States and Japan, but also some of the dynamic nations of the Pacific Rim, particularly Malaysia and Singapore. Putting these latter nations' dynamism together with their investment in education and training, and the low wages paid to many workers, it is not surprising that corporations with bases in the Far East are likely to emerge as new world leaders.

Just as Britain won from the Industrial Revolution, so it may lose in the Information Revolution. Fortunes will again be won and lost. Bill Gates was a drop-out college kid before he saw the future more clearly than his elders, and is now rated the world's richest man. Malaysia may be the Bill Gates of nations, in which case Britain might be the Frank Bruno – a one-time heavyweight past his sell-by date.

There is now cross-party agreement that if the UK is to compete in a global market it must cut public spending to levels comparable with those of its Pacific Rim competitors – which means lower still than the 40 per cent of gross domestic product of today (itself lower than that of other European countries). In order to achieve this, the British government must embrace digital technology to reform the operations of the state.

Kenneth Clarke, Chancellor of the Exchequer in the 1992-97 Conservative government, said that new technology could achieve 12 per cent reductions in the costs of the administration of government.

GOVERNMENT IN THE DIGITAL AGE

Some government advisors believe this understates the potential, which they predict will be nearer 20 per cent. And this excludes savings from the now legalised database matching of government departments such as the Inland Revenue and Department of Social Security, which may cut billions off the welfare bill by catching benefit cheats.

But if British governments have failed to realise the full potential of digital technology, the same can equally be said of most Western governments, including all those within Europe. Despite widespread criticism of the European Commission, it is the Commission that has led the way with a series of important research projects that point the direction for the digital future of government. The inability of national governments to match this vision has led an EC report to state, as late as 1996, that the governments of Europe are unprepared for the challenge of the digital world.

There is no part of our public services that will not be transformed by the digital revolution. From the killing fields of war to the intensive care wards of our hospitals, we will find that new technology will solve many old problems, yet produce new ethical and practical dilemmas. How, when tax evasion is made ever easier through global electronic transactions, are governments to finance their activities? Will central banks retain control over monetary supply and circulation?

There is the question of the ownership of our electronic network. Who should own the infrastructure of electronic kiosks supplying public service information? Will the public demand a one-stop shop not just for public information, but for all their information and transaction needs? How will the public sector be re-engineered and integrated to allow one-stop kiosks to give access to all of the public sector, ranging from every government department, to every local authority and NHS trust?

Unless the politicians and public service managers of today recognise these and other challenges, Britain will be unprepared. The result of this will not merely be that our government will be inefficient, our political

INTRODUCTION

system discredited and the parties unpopular. It will also encourage investment to go into other countries, taking jobs and wealth with it.

This book has been written with those politicians and managers in mind who must accept the challenge, to warn them of the difficulties they face, and to prepare them for the decisions they must take. But it is hoped that students of our political system and the general reader will find it equally relevant. It is written for the technologically uninitiated, in plain language, focusing on those developments that are most likely to succeed.

Over-statement is avoided – it is unnecessary. The reality should be enough to wake the apathetic from their slumber.

❷ Electronic democracy

DEMOCRACY has always been a flawed vision. Even the ancient Greeks who invented it ignored women and slaves when they sought their people's views. Females and the lower classes have been struggling to be heard ever since.

▲ ▲ ▲

For the first time in history, we have the technology to extend the process. We can develop a society that is governed by the people, for the people, with less need for the politician as intermediary. Any question you like could be put to the people and moments later decided upon.

Liberal thinkers can be forgiven for not joining the celebrations. Read the opinion polls about hanging – or even, a few years ago, about race relations – and you realise the potential for conflict between politicians and their electorate. There are many issues where the common view and that of the people's representatives are at variance.

If our society is to have a referendum on every important question, then some useful virtues will be thrown away. Consistency of government policy may be one of the first victims: liberalism may follow soon after.

Uncomfortable dilemmas will soon begin to confront our MPs. If referenda are available instantly, at little cost, very easily, just how often should we have them? If governments turn their back on them, how should politicians treat the referenda that will inevitably be organised by the media?

The tabloid press's enthusiasm for telephone polling must be a pointer for what will happen as interactive TV develops. It is easy to visualise. Sky TV runs a programme on the trial of a particularly despicable child killer and follows it by a poll asking viewers whether the death penalty should be reintroduced.

A large majority agree it should. For the next few days Sky TV, the *Sun* and *The Times* run big news stories about the refusal of MPs to listen to their electors. Each day afterwards there might be an interview with an MP who supports the poll's results, and another who does not. The politicians may stick to their beliefs – but they will need to be strong willed, principled, and willing to be voted out of office.

The trend towards this has already begun. An Internet survey was conducted by Reed, the recruitment service, and found some startling suggestions. One proposal was for all car drivers to have a stake fitted on the steering wheel of their vehicle, to encourage more sedate driving. Another was that MPs should not be permitted to vote unless they have passed a breathalyser test. The better news is that some of the other ideas might be welcomed – the taxing of unhealthy foods and the lining of all motorways with avenues of trees to absorb sound and pollution and reduce their visual impact.

Our attitude to electronic democracy is something we need to decide very soon. Ian Taylor, Conservative minister for information technology until 1997, believed that electronic voting might be introduced in Britain before the millennium. His preference was for its use for the first time in a referendum on a single European currency.

Interactive TV, which would allow any number of 'freelance' votes and opinion polls, is already here. There are trials in operation across the world, including some in Britain, of full two-way TV

GOVERNMENT IN THE DIGITAL AGE

communication. You can already call down video-on-demand in Cambridge as part of its interactive cable TV pilot. And, today, Co-op Bank customers who are connected to Sky TV can view their bank accounts on satellite TV transmissions, while simultaneously issuing instructions on a touch-tone handset down an ordinary phone line.

The most exciting of the trial schemes has taken place in Orlando in Florida, where residents can give their views on the municipal government's latest proposals by responding through their TV screens. The 'Full Service Network' (FSN) serves 4,000 local residents using high quality cable connections (fibre-optic and coaxial) to enable a heavy burden of information to be transmitted – the capacity is 2.5 million times greater than that available on an ordinary phone line. Services available as a result of this higher capacity include video-on-demand, home shopping, games-on-demand, interactive TV and Web TV, which provides access to the Internet and its World Wide Web pages through the TV.

The initiative has been led by Time Warner, and Orlando was chosen as the third largest of its cable networks in the United States. As well as the entertainment facilities there are four strands of public services also available – democracy, culture, health and education, though these are being rolled out sequentially. The education system is to include video-on-demand for home learning. Health TV will allow users to do home health-testing, through organised exercises linked to heart-beat testers, leading to life style advice. GOtv is the culture information service, which gives details of restaurants and leisure activities, complete with booking service.

FSN's Democracy Network is linked to the news-on-demand channel, which is run as a non-partisan guide for viewers, supplying party campaign videos and biographical background on candidates. Responses are available from all candidates on set 'key' questions. This allows participants in local and national elections to vote from home.

ELECTRONIC DEMOCRACY

The scheme is possibly the most advanced of its kind around the world. The Singapore government has examined it with a view to copying it.

As the FSN system develops, it will expand into a more comprehensive home management centre, enabling participants to use it to control their home environment – if necessary from a distance – varying lighting, heating and sound. It could be used to check on security, with burglar alarms connected to personal pagers alerting security guards of a possible intruder. This would then be confirmed by reference to CCTV cameras in the home or small digital cameras spread around the house and networked via the interactive TV. Utility suppliers intend to use similar systems to read meters and offer energy management systems to customers from a distance.

Politicians in parts of the Third World have also reacted favourably to the potential for electronic democracy – at least inside the polling station. Brazil has recognised the need for a more voter-friendly system than paper and pencil if its high proportion of illiterate citizens are to vote. It introduced electronic voting in October 1996, for its municipal elections in the major cities, using PCs for 33 million people to vote on.

Voters had to type in their unique voter number. Electors could then choose a candidate, either from a list of names, or from a list of pictures of candidates. Colour codes and statements of beliefs helped to simplify the process and reduce the risk of votes cast in error. The vote was confirmed by pressing a coloured key, in line with the party's colours. Blind voters were able to use braille keys.

The Brazilian elections did not use network connections, which could have produced the results the moment the polling stations closed. Instead, floppy disks containing the results were collected from each polling station, and counted centrally. Even so, the results were known within six hours instead of the usual month. A prime objective was to reduce the level of fraudulent voting, and the Government is satisfied that this was achieved.

Personal security was effective because the computer system did not cross-reference the voters' identity against their electoral registration number, and votes recorded on floppy disk were protected by double encryption. (This is actually more secure than the system used in Britain, where, theoretically, an elector's voting preference could be traced in a 'big brother' state through the pattern of punched holes on the ballot paper, which represents the voter's electoral registration number.)

The Netherlands, too, uses an electronic voting system. In 1995, half the provincial councils were elected in this way – it was up to the municipalities to decide whether they wanted to use it. Again a requirement by law is that an electronic system must be absolutely secret and secure. The Dutch government believes that the system will more than cover its cost by reducing the staffing of elections. Systems are quicker and more reliable, and can cope with proportional representation, with the potential capacity to handle 126 candidates if necessary. Morocco is among the countries that is considering copying the Dutch system.

Some parliaments, such as that of the European Union, also use electronic voting systems. While these can be operated by elected politicians from their seats in the voting chamber, it is theoretically possible to extend the principle to allow for voting from a distance. This might allow, for instance, MPs who are seriously ill to vote from home, or from their hospital beds, ending the unseemly practice of 'counting in' ambulances containing critically ill MPs.

But these ideas, too, are not politically neutral. Should politicians be permitted to vote even if they have not heard the debate? Do debates in political chambers ever influence a politician's vote? The Liberal Democrat Sir Russell Johnstone has argued that the House of Commons and the European Parliament should permit members to vote from home, to allow MPs and MEPs to miss the dreary and

ELECTRONIC DEMOCRACY

unproductive talking shops, enabling them to get on with constituency work. But would voters believe that politicians really were working if they did not attend the chambers? Would public cynicism against politicians increase further?

MAKING ORGANISATIONS MORE DEMOCRATIC

Less controversial is the potential for improving democracy within organisations. An example is the Local Government Association, the body formed in 1997 to represent all English and Welsh local authorities. Instead of having to convene expensive and time-consuming committee meetings to approve decisions, the LGA expects to introduce widespread electronic consultation.

Many committee meetings may consequently be unnecessary, with all members able to vote, rather than just a few to represent the many. With a highly politically educated membership that already understands in detail almost all issues and questions that might be posed, there is a strong argument that many issues can be addressed by a simple vote from a distance, without the need for members to come together for costly meetings. Some committee meetings will still be necessary, for example to achieve consensus between groups with conflicting views, but the purpose and atmosphere of those meetings will inevitably change.

Like many comparable bodies, the LGA has already discovered the virtue of e-mail. Draft documents can be circulated across the country (or, where necessary, across the world) instantly and for a few pence, and requested changes incorporated.

Local authorities themselves could conduct a similar process. Draft committee papers could be e-mailed to councillors for comments before final publication. But potentially more significantly, ordinary members of the public can have vastly improved access to the workings of their politicians, either through the World Wide Web or via a local authority controlled intranet.

An intranet is a closed network, which uses the technology of the Internet but with firewalls to protect it from unauthorised access. Very few people have access to all of an intranet, and each user will have security clearance only for the information services relevant to them. Ordinary members of the public might automatically be given the right to see all open committee papers, and these could be accessed either from a public access kiosk, or from a home PC connected to the database via telephone lines and a modem.

Several councils have already established networks of this kind. One example is that of Hampshire County Council which operates the Hantsnet system. This is primarily to connect staff, but there are also several information services on-line for the public. These will eventually include publication of committee papers, local weather forecasts, pollution warnings, and a transport information service. Transport information includes details of delays on buses and trains, and road congestion reports. People who subscribe to the system, paying a fee, can consequently plan journeys before they leave home, with the help of their council's information service.

It is likely, though, that the World Wide Web – the open information system of the Internet – will be the main way in which local authorities will in the future communicate with their citizens. Web sites can contain enormous amounts of information about an organisation – some contain millions of pages of information – giving access to whole databases of information. They are also likely to prove far more popular with the public than intranets, which may retain their image of being 'only for the nerds'.

All the big political parties have their own Web pages, and used them to publish details of their press conferences during the last general election. Because the World Wide Web is now interactive, parties also held question and answer sessions with the public at election time. Many central government departments and local authorities have their own Web pages.

Brent council in North London was a pioneer in developing a World Wide Web site. Its entry includes a list of all its councillors, with details of their surgeries; details of forthcoming committee meetings; explanations of the role of councillors, MPs, MEPs and the mayor; and how to make contact with elected representatives. Initially the site did not integrate within it the means of sending electronic mail to councillors and officers, but this will be developed as the site evolves.

As Brent's site matures, it will be linked to a database of recent committee decisions, providing a system of public access to the minutes of council meetings that is much more easily available than the traditional system of wading through files of minutes in public libraries or at the council offices.

Parliaments around the world, too, are moving onto the Web. Australia, Canada, France, Germany and the United States all have parliamentary Web sites containing details on membership, contact arrangements, recent decisions, and the content of debates.

Text of debates in the Houses of Parliament, both in the Commons and the Lords, is also on the Web, at the site 'www.parliament.uk', together with the text of bills being considered by the Houses. The site also lists select committees, and how to contact them, though it does not list the members of the committees, nor does it provide the opportunity to e-mail Members of Parliament.

CONNECTING POLITICIANS

Potentially, digital technology could improve the quality of our democracy, producing a more politically educated population. More information will be available to more people, more easily than before.

GOVERNMENT IN THE DIGITAL AGE

The latest generation of 'search engines' – software that chooses the exact information you want, and rejects the rest – will allow users to be well briefed on the desired topic, while 'push software' will enable parties to send propaganda electronically to its precise target group.

Enthusiasm for the technical possibilities of new technology should not blind us, though, to the political and ethical downsides. There is a real risk of creating what has been termed an 'information aristocracy', with a divide between the 'information poor' and 'information rich' producing a 'magnifying effect' on existing divisions within society.

At the present time it is still a comparatively small section of society that has access to modern technology. Even in the United States, which is far more Internet aware than Britain, nine out of ten homes are *not* on-line – which is both a marketing challenge and an enormous commercial opportunity for the ICT industry. For the moment it would be wrong to restrict the advantages of modern technology only to those groups who have home access to the Internet, or to those who have the education and wealth to understand how to use new technology.

There is consequently a commonly held view that while it is acceptable to allow home PC users to lobby their politicians, it would be wrong – at least until interactive TV is used in most homes, which is likely to be some time after the year 2000 – to allow people to vote in elections from home electronically. (People with disabilities can, of course, already vote by post from home.)

It may be appropriate to phase-in the applications of ICT into the political world, so that its impact can be judged. The respected political commentator Andrew Adonis has argued: "There are huge dangers in electronic democracy, so let us be aware of that, and pioneer it in local government."

But the potential lobbying revolution on politicians through the use of e-mail probably cannot be held back. Electronic mail is easy, quick and very popular. Take a personal example. If I am annoyed with the BBC

ELECTRONIC DEMOCRACY

for dropping a radio programme I had stayed in for, I can instantly send them an e-mail to complain. In truth, if I had to send a letter by surface mail or by fax, or make a phone call to log a complaint, I would not bother. Complaining has never been so easy.

Equally, a generation of people have never before had such quick and easy access to those MPs who have an e-mail address and make that address known. We can assume that most MPs will, willingly or reluctantly, soon be easily contactable by e-mail.

Traditionally, of course, it has mostly been the educated middle classes who complain. And it is precisely that same section of society who buy and use PCs. We can expect an avalanche of lobbying by e-mail to all sorts of organisations, but most especially to politicians and public bodies. This is already happening in the United States where senators and congressmen receive huge quantities of e-mail correspondence.

We might argue that this will improve the quality of service delivery, improve the democratic accountability of services and of our representatives, and be altogether a good thing. This is true up to a point, but overlooks the fact that most of the lobbying will be in a single direction. Politicians will face increasing demands by the well-off, with poorer people unlikely to have the same access or interest.

Ian Taylor, the former Conservative information technology minister, has argued that this is not a problem. Politicians will simply 'discount' this factor, he said, recognising that e-mail lobbying by the middle classes masked the views of many other people without the same access to politicians. Yet it is impossible to understand how views which remain unarticulated can be taken into account. Giving the middle classes an improved means of lobbying their politicians is bound to give the middle classes even more influence.

Advisors to the European Commission (in the first annual report by the Information Society Forum) make the point that new technology will

GOVERNMENT IN THE DIGITAL AGE

improve the ability of pressure groups to organise members' representations, which could further distort the political process.

"The speeding up of the political process may put increased pressure on representative systems," says the report. "Government may become more reactive in style and less considerate of different views and interests. Politicians may become more prone to follow powerful interest groups which have easy access to high technology. There is even a risk of a commercialisation of politics and election campaigns, given modern marketing techniques."

The general perception that computers are only for the young may not be absolutely accurate, but it is more true than untrue. Research conducted as part of the British government's 'IT for All' campaign found that, while one in three men consider the Internet to be useful in their daily lives, only one in six women do. The survey found that the typical PC enthusiast is male, aged between 16 and 34, and a member of the AB higher socio/economic class.

A Manchester City Council report, 'Creative cities and the information society', argued that talk of open participation in a digital democracy was too optimistic. "There is a serious danger that this ignores the realities of power which support an 'information aristocracy' rather than a 'digital democracy'," said the report. "If citizens are not able to have access to the new telematics infrastructures and services, the outcome will simply reinforce existing patterns of inequalities with 'information haves' and 'have-nots' in our community."

This outcome is not inevitable. Despite the narrow cross-section that uses the Web today, steps can be taken to improve interest and access. When Chelmsley Wood library, on a deprived council estate in Solihull, introduced PCs, providing public access and training, it had, for the first time in its history, queues of local people wanting to get in. While many of them were the usual male adolescents, there was also a very high portion of women and older unemployed and retired men – keen to find out what they had been missing.

The Chelmsley Wood experience gives a clear pointer that the right combination of location, training, open access, encouragement and promotion can break down the barriers to the use of digital technology.

Another solution to the problem of narrow access is to increase the relevance and number of multimedia kiosks. We are gradually seeing the spread of kiosks in some public buildings, such as libraries, and rail and bus stations, and, more commonly, in banks and building societies. The new Labour government has also spoken of introducing public information kiosks in hospitals.

Kiosks are interactive terminals, that allow the user to communicate with an organisation without the need to be personally seen. Kiosks are commonly used across much of the world, and will gradually replace the cash machines currently used by banks.

An example of one of the more advanced kiosk systems is that used in Newham in East London, under a pilot scheme led by the European Commission, which involves the local authority, the Metropolitan Police and systems supplier Olivetti. The terminals look much the same as traditional, hole-in-the-wall cash machines, but are touch-screen controlled, with attached telephone, a scanner to read documents, and camera to facilitate video-conferencing.

The kiosks can be used by the public to contact the police to report a crime or suspicious behaviour. They can save people visiting a police station, with motorists who have been stopped being permitted to use them to produce their driving licences, vehicle licences, insurance and MoT certificates through the scanner. People who are on police bail can visit the kiosk as part of the bail conditions, rather than having to go to a police station in person.

Smart card readers are also contained within the kiosks, and residents with smart cards can use the kiosks to check the balance of their council tax accounts, and confirm whether they are entitled to council tax benefit and housing benefit. They can be interviewed by a specialist welfare rights advisor to establish whether there are other benefits they should claim.

There is a network of 13 translators integrated into the system, some based in council offices, others working from home. A high proportion of the local population speaks Bengali or Somali as their first language, while there are also many Chinese, Vietnamese, Hindi and Urdu speakers, and use of the kiosk, with its video-conference facilities, saves the time and cost of having to arrange translators to attend meetings at council offices or police stations. It also means they are on call instantly in the event of a crisis.

Using translators operating from home allows the council and the police to employ them on a freelance basis, paying them only when required, rather than on full time, permanent contracts. As the quality of the cable connections improves, better video-conference images will be possible, which will also allow signers for the deaf to be incorporated into the system.

Newham's system is also being used in other pilot areas in Europe, include Strathclyde, Marseilles and Thessalonika, as part of the Attach network – the Advanced TransEuropean Telematics Applications for Community Help. The EC believes it could form the basis for public service kiosks across Europe. Residents in Newham who have cable TV links can use elements of the system from their own homes, using a handset, similar to a normal TV remote control device, to give yes/no instructions.

BUILDING A DEMOCRATIC CONSENSUS

As well as the major cities, it is often the isolated communities that have responded enthusiastically to the potential of on-line terminals. Electronic Village Halls were established in Scandinavia in the mid-

1980s, often based in village schools. They act as an information resource and inquiry point in sparse rural areas.

The Alaska Legislative Teleconference is another response to similar pressures. These were created in response to the complaints from a diffuse population that attending the chamber was impractical for most of them. The legislature does not merely report on events, but allows citizens to ask questions and make comments. The result is a more inclusive and consensus-building approach from decision-makers.

A further development on the same theme is the QUBE system in Columbus, Ohio, where voters respond via interactive TV to the suggestions and debates from the legislative chamber. This builds on the use of Electronic Town Meetings (ETMs) which have been taking place in some countries for the last 20 years. These attempt to increase active involvement in the discussion of political issues.

In Canada in 1994, the Reform Party led an ETM debate on euthanasia. The party agreed that if over 70 per cent of participants reached a conclusion, it would be binding on the party's MPs. This is what happened, with popular support for people's right to choose to die, and the party accepted this decision despite most MPs taking a contrary personal view. In 1992 Ross Perot ran his United States presidential campaign using ETM to promote his candidacy, and improve contact with voters on what he identified as key issues.

An initiative has also been run in Britain, based on the same principles. UK Citizens' Online Democracy, a non-profit and non-party organisation, ran an open forum for electors and politicians to discuss transport and constitutional issues, with co-operation from all the major parties.

The network of so-called 'European Digital Cities', coordinated by the European Commission, is also proving a useful pilot for how municipalities can offer improvements to democracy, information and service standards. One of these cities is Bologna in Italy, which recognises the risk of what it calls 'the magnifying effect' of speeding up existing trends towards polarisation and fragmentation of society, and the centralisation of government, allied to the risk of new social and political discrimination against those without access to new technology.

The municipality of Bologna has agreed that, for it, 'teledemocracy' must mean the guarantee of existing freedoms of expression, plus an undertaking from the council that it will supply, electronically, all important information affecting its citizens. It also guarantees the right of consumers to be protected from false information, whether commercial or political. The council further believes that these rights must be integrated with a right to work, providing citizens with the income to take advantage of improvements to society.

In practice, for the residents of Bologna, this means that access to the Internet is guaranteed, though not necessarily free of charge. While the city must be effectively cabled to allow citizens to subscribe to a subscription service that provides 'teledemocracy', there is still the risk that economic factors could prevent some people from taking advantage of it. The practical conflict between political aspirations and economic realities is something that Bologna will have to grapple with in the coming years – as will the rest of us.

❸ The legal system

2008

Jim, Phil's nephew, was the least respectable member of the family. He had a history of minor offences after an unruly childhood. Now, at 17, he was well known to the police.

One evening, in his home town of Leamington Spa, he had drunk too much in the pub, and been aggressive on his way home. He had kicked car door panels and smashed shop windows. It was behaviour he was unlikely to have committed had he been sober. He might still have wanted to, but he would have remembered to look out for the CCTV cameras.

Five years before, the council, the police, the Home Office and the private company 'Security is Yours' had reached an agreement for the private financing of a network of CCTV cameras around the streets of Leamington. The company linked its cameras to the police database of criminal offenders, on which photos were digitally analysed to recognise facial features, such as size of nose, distance between eyes, and other facial proportions.

Criminal behaviour caught on CCTV could be automatically matched digitally to the database, and those identified, such as Jim, were mailed summonses the day after the offence. When Jim was sentenced, another day later, he was confined to his home for a month. Because Jim was under 18, his parents were required to pay 1,000 Euros compensation to the owners of the shops and cars damaged by Jim, and a further 500 Euros fine – which went straight to 'Security is Yours' as their fee for administering the case from camera to court.

The court system was fully electronic. The video tape of the offence was shown in court on a wall screen. The shop and car owners were interviewed by videoconference from their workplaces, to save them having to attend court in person. Jim's hearing took just 10 minutes of court time, whereupon he was shackled and sent straight home.

The Criminal Justice Agency, a government quango, told Jim he would be given one hour to get home, before the digital surveillance would be made operational. If he left his home at any point from then on for the next month he would be re-arrested and charged for breach of his sentence conditions.

Monitoring was conducted through a modification to the interactive TV, carried out after a previous conviction, with a sensor to check that Jim stayed within the confines of the home. If he left, the Criminal Justice Agency would be bleeped through the the TV's cable connection and a warrant would be automatically issued for Jim's further arrest.

This arrangement saved a fortune in prison costs, passing the burden of Jim's keep over the next month onto himself and his parents. Jim's mother and father would have to keep him in food – if Jim lived on his own he would have to order food for delivery if he could not get a friend or family member to do it for him. This presented no practical problems, as teleshopping was a standard application on home multimedia units – there were several specialist TV shopping channels which allowed you to buy everything you could conceivably want, and quite a lot else as well.

Prison was now only used for those convicted of the most serious offences, and for that small number of people who persistently ignored home detention orders. These were not universally popular, with some politicians arguing that they were not enough of a punishment or deterrent, but they were generally unpopular with people convicted and their families – which was, after all, the main idea.

▲   ▲   ▲

THE LEGAL SYSTEM

OUR FUTURE LOOKS LIKE SINGAPORE TODAY

IT might be argued that while Jim's experience is already technically feasible, it would not be politically acceptable. Yet much of the court procedure is already being used in Singapore, and the tough line being adopted by British politicians against, in particular, youth offenders, allied to the awareness of the burgeoning costs of prison and youth detention, makes all of the above imaginable.

Singapore is arguably the world's most electronically advanced nation. This is easier for a small island country the size of Singapore to achieve than for many others – the population is three million, and it covers just 400 square miles. It is also a nation of youth, with the average age a mere 32, so that most of the population finds digital technology a natural factor in their lives. The government intends every citizen to have, before the year 2000, his or her own smart card, containing all essential details relating to identification, health, education and insurance.

All Singapore government departments have their own Web sites, and applications to departments can be made electronically for exit visas, government jobs, work permits, and for places in schools and child care centres. A system of e-mail, the 'Government Electronic Mailbox', allows questions to be asked of any civil servant, or to request service improvements. All government offices are connected electronically, including video-conference links, and will gradually be contactable through a network of public access kiosks and through interactive TV in the home.

The Supreme Court publishes on its Web site a list of its judges with their pictures, and details of forthcoming cases. There is an Automated Traffic Offence Management System which brings together the courts with the police and the Land Transport Authority, so that motorists can pay traffic fines and licence fees through the island's kiosks, with the amount payable reduced because of the savings achieved from the electronic system.

Subordinate courts themselves are electronically connected with video-conference facilities, so that defendants do not always appear in person. Prisoners on remand watch the proceedings from their remand prison, through a two-way video-conference link, saving the transport costs of attending the court in person, and removing the risk of an escape.

Some witnesses, such as in rape cases, appear through a video-conference link to reduce the trauma of a court interrogation. Discussions between the judge in chambers with lawyers can also be conducted through a video-conference link to cut the time and cost to lawyers of appearing in person.

In the United States, too, there is increasing use of video-conferencing to reduce the amount of prisoner travel. Where, traditionally, prisoners have sued prisons to earn themselves a day out of jail, the authorities have responded by hearing these cases through video-conference links. This reduces the cost of the hearings; removes the need to transport the prisoner; and will ultimately make it less likely that prisoners will instigate legal action against the prisons.

Singapore's Immigration Auto-Clearance System, which begins operation in late 1997, will speed up the processing of people coming into the country. Immigrants who have been given re-entry visas will be issued with personal smart cards, complete with biometric details – information on the physical appearance of the person, which initially will be restricted to the person's fingerprints, but might be extended to record other features, such as iris image. Using fingerprint scanners and smart card readers it will be possible to speed-up the processing of immigrants to just 10 seconds per person.

The island's police also use electronic communications, through laptop computers connected via radio-wave transmissions. Officers can transmit to headquarters the video pictures of the scene of an incident, and can

THE LEGAL SYSTEM

receive photos and profiles of suspects. It is now standard practice for police officers to compare photos transmitted from the police database with the actual appearance of a person stopped for questioning, enabling the police to know if they have been given correct identification details by suspects, and whether a person is already wanted for questioning.

IN BRITAIN, TOMORROW

Although Singapore is further advanced than other countries in its use of digital technology, many of its applications are likely to become widely copied. In Britain, police forces are phasing-in mobile communication devices that bring together the technologies of mobile phones and lap-top computers, connected by radio-telephony, but with messages scrambled to prevent unauthorised reception or interference.

These devices, like those used in Singapore, will transmit video images from incident scenes and request information on given car registration numbers and names of suspects. They can be attached to printers installed into police vehicles, to give officers print-outs of people wanted for questioning. The new systems should also operate in a much wider geographic area, be subject to fewer 'black holes' where they do not work, than the old police radios, whose technology dates from the 1940s and be less susceptible to criminals listening in.

The Home Office in Britain is in the process of creating a digital computer identification system, which will provide 'facial mapping' of all convicted criminals and wanted suspects on a single national database. These have been trialled by some local police forces, and proved reliable and workable. This will allow any person caught on video to be identified by computer within seconds if their face is already on the database.

Initial priorities will be armed forces bases and airports, to record the presence of any terrorist suspects, and football stadiums, to inform police officers and stewards of the presence of people with convictions for violent disorder. It is expected that a comprehensive digital database, matched to CCTV cameras, will be operational across Britain by the year 2002.

Electronic recording of traffic crime, which triggers the automatic issue of summonses to motorists, is likely to be in place much earlier than this. Digital cameras, which store images without using photography's traditional film and chemical system, are likely to be used in roadside cameras in Britain by the end of 1998, cutting costs and speeding up the transmission of information and images.

Pictures will be taken automatically, triggered when cars exceed a speed limit. Images will be instantly transmitted by way of high quality cable connections, recording the registration number of the vehicle. A central computer, linked to the records system of the Driver and Vehicle Licensing Agency, might automatically and immediately raise a summons against a vehicle's registered owner.

This infrastructure will be expensive to provide, but one option that a government will have to consider will be whether to bring in private finance. A public/private partnership could allow a commercial supplier to provide the digital camera and links with the central database without charge, in return for earning a portion of the generated fines.

Other applications of roadside digital cameras will be targeted against motorists travelling in restricted bus lanes; vehicles being driven the wrong way down one way streets; and drivers going through red lights. Digital cameras on motorways may continuously transmit pictures, helping police investigate the causes of serious accidents and prosecute bad drivers.

There is also a move to require new vehicles to contain black box

THE LEGAL SYSTEM

recorders, possibly connected to miniature digital cameras in front and rear bumpers. These would be used to assess blame in the event of an accident, in the same way that flight recorders in aircraft do. Other black boxes are now used in some types of racing cars. The black boxes might also be inspected on a random basis to ensure that drivers have not been speeding – a natural evolution of the tachograph used in lorries and coaches.

As more advanced software is developed, road side and CCTV cameras will be used for more analytical purposes, using so-called 'artificial intelligence'. There are several types of artificial intelligence software, but broadly they are systems that enable computers to 'think' and to 'understand'. They compare normal behaviour, and recognise the abnormal. By using reference points of previous incidents, they can analyse what is happening, produce an explanation, and issue warnings to appropriate agencies.

Consequently, a driver weaving between lanes of a motorway will, in the future, trigger a computer attached to a roadside camera to issue a warning to nearby police vehicles, and a request to apprehend and arrest. It can also predict road accidents and congestion (see chapter four).

Applications will be much wider than just for road traffic though. Computers connected to CCTV cameras will recognise that defined activities, such as the coming together of large gangs of youths containing people previously convicted of violent crime, can be flashpoints, requiring urgent attendance by police officers.

Artificial intelligence will also be able to predict some major tragedies. The Health and Safety Executive has invested heavily in computer modelling systems to analyse the reasons for recent disasters, such as the Hillsborough football stadium crush, and the Kings Cross fire.

This has allowed the HSE better to understand the reasons for these events, and demand improved safety standards. It has also enabled university software researchers to examine the potential for the use of

GOVERNMENT IN THE DIGITAL AGE

artificial intelligence in computers connected to CCTV cameras, in order to produce warnings when there is a risk of similar events occurring in the future.

These developments may be more significant than they appear. Initially the fire service believed the Kings Cross fire was minor, because the amount of smoke was quite small. Using the results of computer modelling allied to artificial intelligence and CCTV cameras, it would be possible to alert the fire service in the future that a fire might be more serious than it seemed.

Systems within the courts are also being modernised fast. EDS, the US-based computer systems and information services multinational established by Ross Perot, has been contracted by the Lord Chancellor's Department to introduce a comprehensive information and communications system for the British courts. These will instantly provide details in the court of the background to a particular case, and the defendant's criminal record. Judges will refer easily to case precedents, and sentencing policy laid down by senior judges and Parliament.

Legal disputes in the UK are also, again like those in Singapore, increasingly likely to use video-conferencing technology to make expert witnesses more easily, and more affordably, available. This will be of ever more importance as the global character of trade will inevitably create new needs to hear from parties and witnesses who live and work in other parts of the world.

The 1996 government green paper on information and communication technology, 'Government.Direct', also spelled out other potential applications in the legal system, which must be incorporated, alongside other proposed reforms laid down in the Woolf report, to make legal redress more accessible and affordable.

At the most basic level, this will involve public access kiosks that will guide the lay user through the legal system, giving a simple explanation of a person's rights and responsibilities. Initially these kiosks may be

THE LEGAL SYSTEM

dedicated for legal disputes, sited within court buildings, but may eventually be integrated into wider networks of kiosks.

Simple legal actions may be initiated through the kiosks – such as small claims actions or petitioning for uncontested divorce and conveyancing work – as part of the Government's drive to make justice cheaper, easier and more accessible to the lay person. The kiosks would be attached to laser printers, so that appropriate documents could be produced, signed, and lodged with the court there and then. These same kiosks would also be used for the payment of court fees and fines.

BIG BROTHER WATCHES OVER US

It would be wrong to present the application of digital technology to the justice system as being necessarily good, or as uncontroversial. The British lobbying organisation Justice responded to the 'Government.Direct' document by arguing that "new technology can pose new threats to privacy which should be anticipated and guarded against well in advance.... Where the Government itself is the initiator of developments which involve the increased handling and exchange of personal data, there is particular need for caution; information is power, and like all power [it] can corrupt its holder if checks and balances are not in place."

Justice has lobbied for the Data Protection Registrar to be given a statutory role in monitoring changes in law and administrative arrangements, and it has expressed great concern at the use of data-matching between government databases to detect fraud. (See chapter six.)

Others are concerned at the application of global surveillance systems. Essentially these come in two categories – satellite photographic surveillance, and global telephone tapping surveillance.

The left-wing civil rights lobbying group, Statewatch, points out that the European Union and the United States' Federal Bureau of Investigation have agreed a common set of standards for all communication traffic – to cover phones, faxes, e-mail and telexes – which manufacturers must adhere to. It is intended that other trading blocks should sign up to the agreement.

While the stated intention is to monitor serious crime – particularly terrorism, drug trafficking and associated money laundering – Statewatch claims that many governments will find it irresistible to use the technology against less serious crime, such as road protesters, and political dissenters who are not guilty of criminal activity.

A Statewatch report claims that the privatisation of state-owned telecommunications corporations and the replacement of comparatively easily tapped land- and sea-based cables has encouraged governments to seek ways of keeping a check on all satellite communication. The now agreed communications standards will allow governments to continue to monitor targeted individuals or organisations, whose normal communications channels will be 'tagged'.

In addition, key words, names and phrases in *any* phone conversation, or fax or e-mail traffic, may generate automatic logging of the call and subsequent detailed surveillance of the individual. In such circumstances it could be unwise to make certain types of jokes when using telecommunications.

Of course, for people who have lived in the old Soviet bloc, or under other dictatorships, there is little new in any of this. The difference is in capacity and scope. Surveillance will be much easier and more reliable, and unscrupulous governments will find it straightforward to monitor all calls rather than just those of a targeted few.

It is, though, equally important to focus on the potential of digital technology to aid crime and the avoidance of detection. Tax avoidance is a key element of this which will be examined in chapter 11.

There are obvious dangers that the reliance on computers for

THE LEGAL SYSTEM

transactions and accountancy records may make it easier for fraudsters to move money into other accounts, or, in some instances, to hack into other computers to move money.

While successful hackers are always likely to generate press interest, the risk from hacking should not be overstated. 'Firewalls' are necessary to protect confidential information from unauthorised access – remember that each telecommunications line out to retrieve information from the Internet is also a potential line in for someone outside to gain information. But with modern day systems of firewalls, encryption systems and, perhaps most important of all, restricted access based on smart cards plugged into a PC or other terminal, it will be unusual for information to be wrongly obtained.

More worrying to many is the ability of criminals to launder money quickly once it has been wrongly obtained, for example through drug trafficking. Within an hour, a sum of money might easily be transferred through 20 bank accounts, using modern systems of distance banking by PC.

Tax and investigation authorities are developing advanced systems of artificial intelligence software to detect unusual and apparently improper transfers of money. The potential can be seen from the system adopted by the London Stock Exchange, which has installed artificial intelligence software that detects unexpectedly high volumes of selling of shares immediately prior to a price sensitive announcement.

The software automatically instructs the computer to compare the names and addresses of buyers and sellers with those of people employed by the company whose shares are being sold, and other companies that have a close contractual relationship with it, such as its public relations consultants. It is expected to lead to a big step forward in the detection of insider trading.

The big accountancy firms are developing their own software systems that are aimed at following illicit withdrawals and movements of big sums of money. It is hoped that this will detect where a fraudster has transferred money to, by examining the records of a range of banks to examine deposits and withdrawals in order to establish a pattern of dispersal.

However, the success of this approach clearly depends on the willingness of banks to co-operate. It is obvious that many will not. The development of a global economy further underlines the problems caused by trading with banks based in countries that do not accept international conventions on bank regulation and transparency. This applies just as much to Switzerland as it does to some of the small offshore banking islands. The Bank of Credit and Commerce International, for one, would not have co-operated with attempts to trace money fraudulently deposited.

If digital technology promises the hope of solving some of our problems of criminal behaviour it should be equally clear that it throws up new challenges, both in terms of the opportunities it gives for bad governments to become more efficient dictators, and for crooks to avoid detection.

As ever, it will be a contest between the good guys and the bad ones to use the new technology more effectively than the other. There will probably be no clear winner, but we can expect the fight to last a very long time.

❹ Transport

2008

It was 6 o'clock in the morning when Phil's boss phoned him. "Sorry to disturb you so early," he said, "but we've got a crisis with the Tunis packaging plant. Go and sort it out will you."

Phil got out of bed and went down to his interactive TV, to see what transport arrangements he could organise. First he needed to arrange a flight to Tunis. There was one at 7.15 a.m. – it looked like a possibility if he could get to Heathrow in time. Phil checked that there was still a seat available on the plane and there was, at a cost of 350 Euros. He was carefree about the cost as the firm would be paying.

Not surprisingly the timetables said that he could not get to the airport by train or by bus in time for the flight. It also pointed out that he could not drive to the airport in time, because of the time it would take to park his car. The system helpfully pointed out that if Phil went by taxi he should make the plane, as the roads between Phil's home in North London and Heathrow were clear.

Phil used the on-line electronic travel agency network to book the plane seat and order the taxi for 10 minutes time. He agreed to pay in advance for both by approving a deduction from his smart card which he had inserted in the TV's smart card reader. If there had been a train or coach connection he could also have bought tickets for those on the same system, and if he expected to stay overnight in Tunis he could have booked hotel accommodation.

The taxi arrived promptly, giving Phil just enough time to dress, and took him straight to the airport. They got there at 6.50 a.m. – plenty of time. There was no

GOVERNMENT IN THE DIGITAL AGE

need to collect a ticket, because everything had been arranged electronically and the airline's computer system was expecting him. Phil went straight to the ticket barrier, inserted his smart card, put his finger onto the fingerprint reader, and looked straight into the camera so that his face and iris could be checked against his smart card-held identification details. The airport computer interrogated the Home Office's crime database which confirmed that Phil was not convicted or suspected of terrorist activity.

Phil's smart card was like an old fashioned credit card, but with a microchip on the reverse instead of a magnetic strip. The microchip held a vast array of information about Phil. It acted as his identification card, including his passport. It was his payment card, called an electronic purse, allowing him to pay for any transaction, however small, by being inserted into a cashier's till, or into an interactive TV's smart card reader.

The smart card also contained Phil's security clearance for getting into his employer's factories and offices. It was interrogated by on-line computer systems to give him access to some databases, but refuse him access to others. One of the beauties of the smart card was that although it was a computer, complete with processing power, it was completely secure from hackers and software viruses.

Today, at the airport, the smart card was the reason why it took Phil less than 15 minutes from arrival at the airport to get onto his plane. The smart card held his flight booking details, his passport details, his identification confirmation, and his payment status. Phil walked through the gates, through the departure lounge, straight onto the plane, and in a few minutes he was in the air. As the plane took off Phil reflected how strange it was that just 10 years before the procedure could have taken hours to sort out.

▲ ▲ ▲

A TRAVEL REVOLUTION

MANY of the most advanced electronic systems are now available to ease air travel, but the same principles can be applied for other transport means. Distance booking, timetable information, electronic payment and up-to-date detail of delays are

TRANSPORT

relevant for planes, trains, buses, coaches and ferries, and better information systems will provide enormous benefits to drivers of commercial and private vehicles.

Major steps forward have been taken to integrate passports, identification cards and travel tickets, brought together onto smart cards for the frequent traveller. This will significantly reduce the time it takes to book-in for air travel, reducing the real cost for the business traveller. Airlines are increasingly keen to cut passenger delays for domestic as well as international flights, as they face increased competition from high speed, privatised train services.

What is less clear is whether the citizen of the future will have just one smart card for all functions, or whether they will be expected to carry different smart cards for each of our many regular activities. The advantage of doing this is that if we lose a smart card, it would only disrupt a single activity – rather than dislocating our entire life until a replacement is obtained.

Smart card suppliers, such as Motorola, want to see multi-purpose smart cards adopted. This makes obvious sense as each small plastic card can have as much data stored on it as entire computers were capable of 30 years ago. It is also highly attractive to financial services companies, which want to 'rent out' spare capacity on bank-issued credit and debit cards.

This is no academic debate for the distant future. London Underground may have a smart card system for the payment of journeys in place of individual tickets up and running by 1998. Phone call boxes use plastic cards that in some instances are themselves smart cards. In many countries across the world smart cards are used in place of cash – in Siberia and Nigeria, for example, where plastic cards are safer to carry than cash. The pilot scheme in Swindon of the Mondex electronic purse has run since 1995.

Smart cards are just one element of the electronic revolution that will

GOVERNMENT IN THE DIGITAL AGE

change the character of journey planning. The latest generation of software can search Web pages to find the cheapest flight, the earliest departure, or the best recommended hotel, to help consumers booking holidays and business trips. This software uses 'intelligent agents', or 'bloodhounds', to go out on the Web and find what the buyer wants.

Advanced electronic travel information systems will also have a major impact. They are already becoming commonplace, especially for those of us who use the London Underground regularly. The same principles used to advise us of forthcoming tube trains, and of delays, can be used for a range of other travel information.

Southampton and Birmingham have electronic displays at bus stops on some routes, advising when the next bus is expected, and how long any delays will be. Buses within these schemes carry electronic identification devices, which are read by scanners sited at the side of the road or by satellite tracking. The scanners detect which service the bus is on, and communicate to the electronic displays at following bus stops the expected time of arrival of that bus, complete with destination details. This helps passengers to decide whether it is worth waiting, or if they should make alternative arrangements.

This system has other applications. On one occasion a Birmingham bus was stolen, but its electronic identification gave its position away enabling the bus to be quickly tracked and recovered, and the thief arrested. Digital signals can also be used to change traffic light signals, helping buses to gain priority over cars at congested junctions. Even more importantly, they can give emergency vehicles priority at traffic lights, improving response times to emergencies, and reducing the risk of accidents by eliminating the need for them to go through red lights.

We are gradually beginning to see a more comprehensive network of electronic transport information which connects with the Web, closed intranet systems and kiosks sited in bus and train stations and in other public places. It is not surprising that this is happening: the question is rather why did it not happen sooner?

The technology has been around for years, but it has been very slow to be used effectively or comprehensively. The problem has been one of cost, with implementation hampered by the privatisation of trains and buses. For years, it was only possible to make on-line enquiries about British Rail trains by looking at the Europe-wide timetable that the German train operator had placed on-line through Compuserve.

Although it was technically practical to establish a network of multimedia kiosks in rail stations, where passengers could check on train connections, look at delays, and buy tickets, there was no money to pay for it. British Rail, before privatisation, said that it would not invest in them because it did not believe it would generate additional ticket sales.

CONGESTION MANAGEMENT

Electronic signalling systems also have applications to help the flow of car traffic. Leicester, for instance, has electronic notice boards around the city advising which car parks have parking spaces. The detection of traffic congestion, through roadside or satellite cameras or by traffic flow monitors on the surface of the road, can trigger changes in priorities at traffic lights, helping to ease traffic densities.

Congestion mapping is also being developed to create a warning system to help route planning. Some new cars are to be fitted with electronic route planners that give advance warning of traffic jams, suggesting alternative routes. They will also give warning signals of major accidents, telling drivers to slow down to avoid them, or to divert to other roads.

Access to the same congestion mapping systems, combined with weather reporting and prediction, will be accessible from the home or office, helping drivers to plan journeys in advance. This can help people to decide whether to travel by car or by train for instance, as well as to choose between roads.

An elementary version of this is provided by Hampshire County Council on its Hantsnet intranet system, which is available to staff, other public sector bodies, and to residents who subscribe. While the initial system only details some transport problems within the county, the council intends it eventually to be integrated into a national transport planning system that contains details of train, road and bus conditions, and weather reports.

Another important element of congestion management will be the use of smart card-based systems for toll payment. It seems increasingly likely that across the European Union there will be a move towards linking taxation to policy objectives, such as the 'polluter pays' principle. This is likely to lead to more taxation levied on car drivers, particularly through road tolls.

In many European countries it is normal to pay tolls to use motorways – indeed the Dartford tunnel and bridge in England have used tolls for many years, and the bridge to the Isle of Skye is also tolled. The new Labour government seems to have accepted the principle of toll charging in Britain. Design, build, finance and operate contracts were awarded by the Conservative government to private construction companies on the basis of payment by 'shadow tolls' – the Department of Environment, Transport and the Regions pays the construction and management contractor on the basis of the number of vehicles that use the road, even if drivers are not charged a fee.

The DETR has already conducted a series of in-depth trials to examine how well smart cards can work for paying tolls. The aim is to have a workable system that electronically deducts a toll fee from a vehicle as it passes a trigger point, without the need for drivers to slow down. Trials have worked well, and it is likely that systems can be in place by the year 2002 – if politicians give it the go-ahead.

TRANSPORT

While electronic tolling meets many political objectives – it can help to manage congestion and pollution, and can be used flexibly to reduce demand at periods of peak congestion or peak pollution by varying charges – it is a subject of enormous political sensitivity. Motorists may react very badly to paying for something they have traditionally used for free. It is probably inevitable, though, if politicians genuinely want to shift people from private to public transport.

There is already in place a network of pilot toll schemes to observe how tolls affect driver behaviour. The British pilot scheme is in Leicester, where participating motorists are given an 'allowance', which they can spend by driving into work every day, or by driving to the edge of the city and commuting in on a 'park and ride' scheme and saving some of the allowance, or by taking public transport all the way from home, and saving even more of the allowance. Leicester's toll system is being implemented alongside changes in traffic priority to reduce journey times for bus passengers, while increasing them for motorists.

New vehicles are beginning to contain smart management systems, reducing pollution emission and improving energy efficiency. More advanced systems will control emissions in urban areas, and switch between the use of petrol or diesel powered engines and a second electric engine for use in cities – the battery will be re-charged by digital management systems using the dissipated energy lost under braking. The smart control systems will 'read' speed limits, and prevent vehicles being driven illegally fast.

Grand prix racing cars have developed smart management systems to a very fine degree, though some of the technology has now been made illegal to prevent it becoming more important than driving skill. These smart systems can be programmed to select gear changes according to the level of load on the engine and the road speed, to eliminate wheel spin, and to detect problems with the car, such as an oil leak, a flat tyre, shortage of petrol or an electrical fault. These same applications will increasingly be employed on road vehicles.

Voice activation systems will be employed in cars to recognise authorised drivers, and fingerprint readers might be used in place of keys to unlock a car, and release the steering wheel. Drivers may be required to pass a simple co-ordination test, to ensure they are not disabled by alcohol or other drugs from driving competently.

As cities move towards becoming 'car free', some municipalities, including Edinburgh council, are keen to run shared pools of cars. One problem of car share schemes is the complex booking and charging arrangements they involve. Tying them into a system of smart card authorisation, and electronic booking from home PC, interactive TV or kiosk, would make them much more manageable.

A member of a council-run shared car pool could book the use of a car through a municipal intranet. They would be told which car they would use, what time to collect it, and from where. Their smart card would unlock the vehicle. At the end of the trip the mileage charge would be deducted from a float held on the smart card.

A similar application for using smart cards to unlock bicycles in shared pool schemes has been developed by Portsmouth University for its students. Until now, councils that have established pools of bikes have found the schemes unworkable because of the number stolen.

The European Commission has taken a strong lead in promoting the development of electronic technology to improve transport systems. It has funded a number of pilot schemes, bringing together equipment manufacturers, public transport operators and local authorities, to see which schemes have wider application.

EC pilot schemes include Chauffeur, which aims to develop automatic distance traffic control, in order to increase the density of freight traffic that roads can handle; Promise, to provide continuing information to travellers during a journey by public or private transport; and Infopolis, to create a single standard for public transport information systems.

TRANSPORT

Part of the EC's emphasis has been to promote telework – working from home or from a distant office, using telecommunications connections – to reduce the need for commuter traffic. (See chapter 10.) Another consideration is to spread the start and finish time of municipally-employed commuters, and to introduce variable toll charges as a tax-led inducement to spread traffic demand for private sector commuters.

This emphasises the reality that traffic and transport policy is as much dependent on fiscal mechanisms as it is on the use of new technology. Smart systems, though, can help to implement those taxation policies, as well as – for the first time ever – operate much more discriminating transport priority systems. The politicians' influence on our transport choices may be about to reach an all time high.

5 Health

2008

A few years earlier, when Phil had difficulty breathing, he went to his GP. "You have asthma," explained the doctor, "so I will give you an inhaler and we will need to monitor it. Don't get too worried about it, but you will have to change your life style a bit, stop smoking and reduce your weight."

The GP then prescribed a regime of daily exercise aimed at reducing Phil's weight at the gym round the corner from Phil's office. Each lunch time after he got better, Phil hooked himself up to a breathing monitor, and did a regulation five miles in 30 minutes on the bicycle machine. The results were automatically reported by e-mail to the GP's surgery, where any abnormality was considered.

Phil had initially been a bit alarmed about the diagnosis, but his doctor had calmed him. The GP then asked Phil to watch a video which explained the problem with Phil's breathing. There was no need for the GP to give Phil a video – Phil simply called it up on the health and life style TV channel's video-on-demand service. The printer attached to the TV printed out suggestions on diet and exercise which Phil stuck to.

Today, though, Phil's exercise regime went unpleasantly wrong. He was tense after a row in the morning with his boss, and he was aware that the air outside was heavy. Now, riding the bike seemed harder work than usual, he was having difficulty catching his breath and began suffering some sharp chest pains. Then the electronic display gave out a series of red flashes and severe respiratory readings. A message told

HEALTH

Phil he should stop cycling immediately.

Within five minutes an ambulance crew had arrived, taking Phil to hospital. The electronic message sent to his GP, whose computer was part of the same health care network as the local hospital, had indicated that Phil had suffered a punctured lung and an ambulance crew had automatically and instantly been alerted.

By the time Phil's GP was aware that there was a problem Phil was already in a hospital bed, plugged into breathing apparatus and other monitoring devices. He was told there was nothing seriously wrong but they had inserted a tube into the side of his chest to re-inflate his lung.

The hospital, of course, had Phil's complete life medical history recorded on its computer system. If someone who was visiting from overseas fell ill in the area, they would be carrying a smart card giving details of their health history, and their health insurance membership, which would be read by the hospital's computers.

While Phil was lying in the hospital bed, feeling a bit of a fraud, a familiar face and voice looked down at him from the video-conference screen. It was his GP. "You're not looking too bad," said Dr Berry, "but this can happen in people who have asthma." Dr Berry always liked to make contact in this way. It gave him an idea what condition his patient was in, and it helped to comfort the patient as well. Soon after Dr Berry had finished, the hospital's lung consultant came to see Phil. The consultant explained he wanted a second opinion, and he called up a specialist in the lung hospital in central London, who asked Phil a few questions and seemed satisfied there was no serious problem. After a couple of days of further monitoring in the hospital, Phil was discharged. He was told that he must stop smoking if he wanted to get better and should stay at home for a few days. He was given a modified exercise regime to adopt after a period of rest. Phil was unsure whether to be relieved or worried, but he knew that if it had not been for the new technology it might have taken a lot longer to recover from the attack.

▲ ▲ ▲

TELEMEDICINE

TELEMEDICINE is not so much science fiction, as science fact. Diagnosis, consultations and case conferences by videoconference are now a reality. X-ray pictures, pathology slides, electrocardiograms and medical records can all be transmitted from one computer terminal to another, accompanied by live discussions between expert consultants on how to treat a patient.

A system of electronic house calls has already been established in Georgia, in the United States. Elderly patients with chronic conditions that need frequent observation, such as heart disease, diabetes and asthma, can attach themselves to computers that are fitted with videoconference equipment, including not just camera and microphone, but also stethoscope and blood pressure cuffs, which can be remotely controlled by a doctor or nurse, and weight scales, thermometer and electrocardiogram.

Consultations, performed daily with some patients, are transmitted through interactive TV links on a local cable TV network. GPs no longer have to visit patients so often, while the patients receive good quality consultations more frequently than before, without having to leave their own homes.

A variety of consultations can take place using telemedicine, creating a new category of words to enter the medical dictionaries, including 'teleradiology', 'telepathology', 'teledermatology', 'teleoncology' and 'telepsychiatry'. Eventually we are likely even to see 'telesurgery', using keyhole technology combining micro-cameras and miniature incisions, overseen by surgeons working through video-terminals from the other side of the world.

Pregnant women can be given ultrasound tests using equipment fitted to computer terminals attached to telecoms links to eliminate the

HEALTH

need for them to visit a hospital for a scan – which is particularly useful for women living in rural areas a long way distant from specialist antenatal units. In the near future, distance monitoring of diabetes sufferers will be possible based on observation of a patient's retina, using high definition cameras and video-conference equipment.

Some of the benefits of telemedicine are obvious – it should help doctors manage their time better; allow specialists to be used for more consultations; and reduce the waste and cost involved in travel. It should also reduce waiting times to see specialists, allowing earlier diagnosis and treatment, increasing the likelihood of survival in a range of illnesses, especially cancers.

Telemedicine can also overcome a number of the disadvantages attached to geographic isolation, and allow centres of excellence to be more easily accessed from distant regions. It seems likely that telemedicine will eventually be adopted in Britain, at least to connect GP surgeries with specialists, with local hospitals, and local hospitals with centres of excellence. Surgeons at Ipswich hospital are sending instant images of endoscopies to specialists for a second opinion. Meanwhile, East Anglian ambulance crews have pilot tested video links with their accident and emergency departments, to help hospitals prepare for patients who are on their way to casualty.

During the Yugoslav civil war, the United States' military paramedics collected the injured from the battlefields and the minefields, with video cameras attached to their safety helmets. Images were instantly transmitted, via satellite technology, to surgeons in the war zone hospitals, allowing instructions to be given to the paramedics.

On some occasions the request was to take the patient to hospital urgently, on another it was keep the patient as still as possible – minimal disturbance is more important than speed when there is the risk of serious spinal damage, for instance. In some cases the paramedics had to undertake cardiac massage where the patient lay, under the expert

GOVERNMENT IN THE DIGITAL AGE

guidance of a doctor at the other end of the satellite video link.

There were even some cases where the surgeons out in Bosnia were short of relevant experience. Telecommunications links were established to specialist surgeons back in the United States so that the best advice and guidance could be given during an operation. The 'global village' created by modern telecommunications links could have no clearer illustration.

Computers can also be used to provide basic diagnosis. Software is being developed that will enable doctors to feed symptoms into their computers and possible diagnoses will emerge. The databases will suggest to doctors some extra questions that could be asked to rule in or out possible illnesses. Computer testing of patients suspected of mental illness found that computers can produce the correct diagnosis in the majority of cases – and as often as psychiatric nurses.

There remain, though, practical problems – as well as cultural and organisational barriers – in using video-conferencing that is combined with the use of diagnostic equipment. It needs high quality telecommunications links, which are currently not generally available. While an ordinary video-conference link can take place through a single ISDN (integrated subscriber digital network) line, the more advanced telemedicine applications, transferring a high quantity of information simultaneously, need 16 ISDN links.

At present this means that ATM (asynchronous transfer mode – not automated teller machines, which are cashpoints), high speed, high quality cable connections are required for advanced telemedicine. The need for this may be overcome as technology and non-cable telecommunications links, especially using radio-wave systems, further evolve.

A more practical alternative to video-conferencing, which is likely to be more popular, at least in the short term, is the use of 'store and forward' records, which transmit information via electronic files,

HEALTH

transferring messages more slowly, therefore needing less high quality telecoms links.

INFORMING THE PATIENT

Electronic communication systems promise to be as relevant to patients as they are to doctors. This is in tune with a growing belief within society, especially among the young, that individuals have the primary responsibility for their own health care. Some Web sites are already being developed aimed at informing patients how to keep fit, take care of their health, and how to diagnose illnesses, while some existing Web sites are targeted at patients, giving support to people suffering from illnesses ranging from cancer to various mental illnesses.

Meanwhile, Glasgow University has developed the Healthpoint touch-screen kiosk, sited in public buildings, to answer a range of patients' questions. A key benefit of Healthpoint and other electronic information systems is in dealing with problems that patients may find too embarrassing to seek advice on otherwise. These concerns may include questions from youths about drug use and contraception, or about AIDS and other sexually transmitted diseases. Available topic areas which people may also be reluctant to speak to their GPs about include prostate troubles, bed wetting and piles.

Other pilot projects involve GPs giving patients videos and CD-Roms to view at home. One study found that patients typically remember only 20 per cent of what they are told during a five minutes consultation with their doctor. Using a video or CD-Rom, patients can have as much as 45 minutes of detailed advice, which they can view in a relaxed environment at home, watch repeatedly, accompanied by relatives or friends, with the patient free to make notes. As the technology develops, integrated into an interactive TV, it will be possible for patients to select option questions for answering.

An alternative, which is already operational, is the use of Patient Information Leaflets, contained on a CD or CD-Rom database which GPs can purchase and print-out from at their surgeries for patients to take home and read. Some GPs based in deprived areas have also established welfare rights databases, giving patients advice on state benefit entitlements. The belief of participating medical practices is that for many patients the best medical help they can be given is extra money to improve their diet and living conditions.

Where interactive TV trials have been established, including in Orlando in the United States and in East Anglia, TV channels have been provided on health and lifestyles. These show programmes about a range of health issues, and offer a video-on-demand service responding to particular illnesses, and to assist patients with self-diagnosis. Whether self-diagnosis will improve patient help or encourage hypochondria – or even lead to greater stress and more ill-health – will only be revealed by experience.

Patients in the future may be given a recovery programme that is agreed jointly between GP and patient, which it is the duty of the patient to oversee. The patient would agree a diet, drug and exercise regime, and personally monitor the effects in terms of both symptoms – through the monitoring of pulse and blood pressure, for instance – and in fitness.

Health policy may also be influenced by interactive TV. The growing debate on rationing of health care has no obvious answer – the demand for costly treatment will obviously continue to grow. Instead of denying that rationing does take place, as British politicians generally do, it will be more practical to have an informed and interactive public debate on how to set priorities.

In one instance a doctor at Guy's hospital in London devised and ran a computer programme to predict which patients would live and which would die following a course of treatment. Had such a programme been found to have worked, and had research been conducted into the value of it, then computer predictions might have informed the debate on when health care should be denied, and where it is best focused. Instead, the experiment caused outrage and there was a straightforward rejection of the principle of using computer models to predict life expectancy, as if humanity was passing responsibility for difficult decisions over to machines.

If politicians do want the public's view in detail on complex moral issues, such as when an ill person should be helped to live and when they should be assisted to die, then interactive TV offers this opportunity.

TRAINING MEDICAL STAFF

Digital technology is increasingly being used to assist the training of surgeons through 'virtual reality'. A life size doll, complete with internal organs, has been manufactured for the Bristol Medical Simulation Centre, attached to the University of Bristol, controlled by a highly advanced computer. Trainee surgeons, assisted by trainee nurses and trainee anaesthetists, can perform mock operations, with the dolls capable of 'resuscitation' if the right steps are taken, or which 'die' or 'relapse' if the wrong action is taken. Simulated road accidents are being used to train paramedics.

Health service managers are attracted by simulation exercises, not only to improve the training of medics and the quality of care, but also because it is expected to have a financial pay-back in terms of fewer negligence claims.

Interactive TV can also be of direct benefit to health care professionals. The cable network of New Brunswick in Canada has a TV channel called Health*Net, which is also a Web page, and which enables hospitals to transmit X-ray images and health care information as a training aid for doctors and nurses.

Several Web sites operate to provide specialist expertise for GPs to access, including one, DocGuide, that acts as a discussion group for doctors to give advice on cases and to request information.

MANAGING THE HEALTH SERVICE

Alas, in Britain at least, computerised information networks have not matched their technical capabilities. The driving force should be there – not just the potential for enormous improvements in health care, but also the prospect of major cost savings.

Much of this might have already been achieved in Britain, but for some terrible mismanagement within the National Health Service. In the late 1980s and early 1990s, the NHS gave generous grants to GPs to purchase computers. At the same time, a partially integrated NHS became more diffuse as the 15 regional health authorities were abolished, and independent NHS trusts took over the running of hospitals. The old centralised NHS computer supplier was no longer the required contractor for hospital trusts, which had the power to make their own purchasing arrangements.

The result was a mismatch of incompatible computers and computer systems across the country. This has held back by years the moves towards an NHS network of networks, linking databases together to provide up-to-the-minute electronic patient records and on-line resource material. Although NHSNet does now exist, and the NHS Executive believes it could save the service £100m a year if generally used, many GPs are reluctant to connect to it because in many cases it would involve replacing computer systems. Even moves to create NHSWeb, a Web site giving all doctors the latest research information, have been dislocated

HEALTH

by the problem of incompatibility and non-cooperation.

Problems have been made worse by disagreements about security arrangements. The British Medical Association believes that the NHS security controls are inadequate, leaving personal patient records too liable to be hacked into. It wants to see higher encryption standards and stronger firewalls used to protect the system from hackers.

But the general move in medicine towards evidence-based treatment can be assisted by a greater emphasis on knowledge, up-to-date information and easy reference to the results of trials and research.

It appears inevitable that our health service will move towards what has been termed a 'hospital without walls', giving rapid information flows to all parts of the NHS. It is certainly the stated objective of advisors to the European Commission who believe that health care networks, linking GPs, hospitals and social centres, should be established to provide less costly and more effective treatment. But the advisors believe that creating an electronic infrastructure will be beyond the budgets of European governments, and should be provided by the private sector, including insurers.

Among the electronic applications envisaged by the European Commission's advisors are the booking of hospital places by GPs; the submission of claims to insurers for the cost of treatment; and the matching of transplant donors with waiting patients. One of the savings that could be achieved is in the faster payment by insurers to hospitals and other treatment providers. Savings can also be achieved through electronic prescribing, improving the quality of prescriptions, reducing the bureaucracy involved, and making fraud and theft of drugs more difficult.

Other advisors to the European Commission, the Information Society Forum, have proposed the creation of a single pan-European library for telemedicine, bringing together from across Europe all research and reports, training materials, and catalogues for schools and universities.

It should network, they suggest, all European hospitals, physicians, medical and pharmaceutical laboratories and social security agencies, and include the medical records of all citizens in the European Union.

The advisors point out that among the problems to be overcome if this is to be achieved is the need to agree a common language for communication, which is likely to be resisted by some member countries.

Britain has moved slower in the use of smart cards (see chapters four and six) than have the United States, France, Japan and Norway. People in effect carry with them their own medical records on a microchip. While the information held on a smart card duplicates that held in hospital and surgery computers, networked across their whole country's health service computer system, it does mean that it can be read and acted upon across much of the world, as well as used for authentication in a patient's own country.

Digital technology can also have a role in updating the old time and motion studies. Hospitals in both the United States and in Britain have used barcodes – which look identical to the barcodes on a can of beans in the supermarket – to study how employees spend their time. Each patient, each nurse and each activity is allocated a barcode, and each nurse given a barcode pen. Nurses swipe the pen on the barcode for each activity they undertake, creating what are called 'data-wells', which are translated into computer databases.

Computer analysis of these databases produces a clear picture of how nurses spend their time, and what the real cost to a hospital is of each patient, and each type of treatment. Equally, the quality of performance of each nurse can be evaluated, and pay adjusted accordingly if the hospital so wishes.

Administrative savings and efficiency improvements underline a lot of the developments underway in the health sector. It has been estimated that between 10 and 20 per cent of the health budgets in the UK and the US could be saved through better use of ICT. It is, of course, a

HEALTH

different question whether once that money was saved the public would want it returned to them through tax cuts or used to improve the quality of health treatment.

Obviously a large proportion of those savings can be achieved by reductions in administrative costs, reductions in drug bills resulting from improved information flows and from the move towards evidence-based treatment, using analysis conducted through computers to determine which treatments work best.

Yet the truth is that in both Britain and America, the proportion of budgets spent on ICT is much smaller than is spent by commercial organisations. Where banks spend 15 per cent of their revenues on ICT, the figure for the US health sector, including the private sector, is under three per cent. The ICT industry believes that improved marketing could lead both to greater sales and to major savings for health care providers.

The problem is that when all of your revenue budget, and far more, can easily be spent on your core activity, it is extremely difficult to justify expenditure that may reduce your immediate ability to do your job. But without a commitment to building a better ICT infrastructure, the longer term efficiencies are not being achieved.

Conservative governments of the 1980s hoped they had solved this problem by pushing the management of hospitals to an arms-length relationship, with the establishment of trusts to run them, but the same pressures have continued to be felt, and the problems of inadequate long term management were perpetuated. The need to create an effective ICT infrastructure for an integrated National Health Service can no longer be delayed.

❻ The welfare state

2008

Phil's mother Sarah would be 62, retiring age, in a few weeks time. It was important to sort out her pension entitlement, so Phil went round to see her one evening to help her complete the electronic form.

Sarah inserted her smart card into the smart card reader on Phil's parents interactive TV, and she selected the lifestyle TV channel. The channel gave her a series of options, and she chose the 'personal finance' one. Another batch of multiple choice icons appeared on the screen, and she opted for 'retirement planning control'.

Her smart card and the computer databases she was now communicating with knew she was coming up to retirement age, of course, but it was Sarah's choice when she actually started drawing her pensions.

As part of the benefits rationalisation programme introduced a few years before, the Government had contracted-out the running of pensions administration to the private sector. For the most part, this meant that the companies running private schemes were also responsible for their clients' contributions into the state system, and, upon retirement, the Government made pensions payments not to the individual, but to the company responsible for most of their private pensions cover.

One of the advantages of this privatisation was that individuals dealt with just one organisation to arrange payment of both their state retirement pension entitlement and their private pension allowance. This company would also, unless the client asked them not to, determine whether the individual had an entitlement to any means-tested state benefits.

THE WELFARE STATE

Unfortunately, this meant that when someone applied for their pension it was a complicated process, which could involve the individual sitting in front of the interactive TV filling in the electronic form for as long as an hour. Because elderly people sometimes had problems with this, they could opt for the guidance of a pre-recorded video-conference link, with an assistant from the pensions company 'suspended' in the corner of the TV screen to explain anything that was confusing. If even this did not help, a real person could be called up on a live video-conference link to answer more complex questions.

In many families, the son or daughter helped parents complete the forms – which was what Phil was doing today. Sarah, helped by Phil, set a date on which she would leave work and would start drawing a single weekly payment, paid by her private pension provider but including her state retirement pension and any other state benefits that she may be eligible for.

Payments could be made in one of three ways to Sarah. Her bank account could be automatically credited by electronic payment, a direct credit; or she could draw her pension by going to a kiosk run by one of the banks or supermarkets, to withdraw her payment onto her electronic purse; or she could withdraw the payment onto her electronic purse through the interactive TV in her own home.

John, Phil's dad, preferred to draw his pension – he had retired a couple of years before – from a kiosk. Although this was less convenient, it did give him an excuse to leave the house. It also entitled him to special offers laid on by the banks and supermarkets that ran the kiosks. One week it would be cheap wine, another week it would be a discount on a foreign holiday. With home shopping so popular these days the banks and supermarkets were forced into special offers to keep customers coming in to see them.

Most of the kiosks were run by supermarkets, as many of the banks had been forced out of business years before by competition from the big supermarkets for their trade. It was now possible to go to one of these kiosks and buy almost anything you wanted, from baked beans to a mortgage. As well as having a smart card reader, they also had a fingerprint reader to confirm your identity, and a camera that would examine your iris and general facial features as additional safeguards against fraud. It was said that the chances of getting away with benefits fraud were less than one in a million.

▲   ▲   ▲

GOVERNMENT IN THE DIGITAL AGE

THE SELF-SERVE SOCIETY

ONE of the greatest efficiency-enhancers of the 20th century has hardly been remarked upon. What other people used to do for us, we now do for ourselves.

We walk around the hypermarket, pulling the items we want from the shelves, and put them into our baskets. We are even beginning to scan the packages as we place them into the baskets so that we can do without the check-out staff as well as the shop assistant.

Our tax liability, once painstakingly analysed by Inland Revenue staff, is now 'self-assessed' – we calculate it ourselves, and it is merely checked on a random basis, partly by computer. (Mind you, the problems suffered by the Inland Revenue introducing the system are a warning about the disruption that can be caused by introducing both a complex new system and additional computerisation of function simultaneously.)

A few years ago, we wrote cheques out by hand, handed them over to a clerk at the counter of the bank, and they were entered up on the computer in the back office to deduct from the balance on our account. Now, we may withdraw money from our account through a cash machine, do our own data inputting on the key board as we go. Or we may pay by plastic with the value electronically and instantly deducted from our account, using electronic point of sale systems. Or we may pay by cheque, and the figure is electronically scanned by the bank during clearance, using handwriting recognition software that is more reliable than the human eye and hand.

Two trends are clear to see. Computers, aided by 'intelligent' software, can do ever more of the things we used to do ourselves, more cheaply and more reliably. And the services we used to pay assistants to do for us we are increasingly doing for ourselves.

The state has been slower than the private sector to pick up on both these trends, especially on persuading the customer to go 'self-service'.

THE WELFARE STATE

Self-assessment is a significant step in this direction, but there is little doubt that a range of other applications will follow. In the UK, benefit applications forms are written by hand, and the information is keyed in by other, employed, hands.

We can expect in the near future that applications will either be electronically completed by claimants, or else that they will be hand-written but scanned electronically. Either way, they will then be assessed by computer, on the basis of past national insurance contributions and means-tested qualification. The result will be a big loss of jobs in the Benefits Agency and the Contributions Agency.

Self-assessment connected to computerisation of calculations should lead to a reduction in errors. Under the current system, the DSS makes errors in 17 per cent of its transactions with claimants – an error rate that would be unacceptable in the financial services industry.

Similarly, there will be no need to employ ticket sellers at train stations, or to have bus drivers delay journeys by selling tickets, once electronic ticket selling and inspection, and the use of smart card prepayment, is introduced. Local authorities will not need to employ staff to receive council tax contributions or housing rent, with payment halls fitted instead with machines that accept cash, cheques and plastic cards.

We can see the trends towards these outcomes across much of the world. In Illinois in the United States, a pilot scheme called 'Touch Illinois' involves applicants for unemployment insurance payments and those wanting to register for job vacancies inputting their own details on electronic direct access terminals. This has greatly reduced the amount of data inputting that staff have to do, while clients are satisfied because they feel more in control of the process, giving them greater flexibility and information.

In the north London council of Brent, applications for housing benefit are scanned onto the computer system. At present, the information contained on forms is not converted into database files, but

GOVERNMENT IN THE DIGITAL AGE

is merely stored as an image in the authority's central computer filing system, called a 'data warehouse'. Elsewhere, for example at the Drivers and Vehicle Licensing Agency, advanced handwriting recognition software allows forms to be 'read' and the information stored and used by the computers.

As well as reducing the amount of data inputting, moving to direct access for clients will also reduce the need for customer support by staff. Finland, which has one of the highest Internet usage rates per capita in the world, expects that establishing an Internet enquiry system will eliminate half of the government's paperwork, and half of its telephone enquiries.

Newham council in east London has a trial scheme of kiosks, where residents can enquire about progress on benefit claims, applications for council housing, requests for planning permission, or else complain about their dustbin not being emptied.

Every aspect of dealing with the customer will be affected by this trend. State benefits will no longer need to be paid through the mailing of cheques or order books in the post, with the ensuing delays and risks of theft.

In Texas in the United States, welfare payments are made to three million claimants by crediting food tokens to plastic cards that can only be used after users key in their personal identification number (PIN). The credits must be exchanged in food stores for family food. As the cards were introduced sales of food increased and those of alcohol dropped. All of America's states must introduce similar systems by the year 2002.

South Africa has seen a simultaneous racial and political revolution, alongside a technological one. The private banking sector has been working with the government to provide services to the black population, many of whom cannot read or write. Welfare payments are accessed by 'electronic benefit transfer' through smart cards that are used at the banks' cash machines. Identification is confirmed by use of sensors to read fingerprints. The device also contains a pulse reader, so that if a

THE WELFARE STATE

thief cuts off the finger of a person entitled to benefit – and this has happened – the thief cannot withdraw any money.

The cash machines are connected to the bank's central computer system using satellite and radio-wave communications, so that cash machines can be sited in the bush or in townships, without cable connections to the main cities.

In Britain, through the ICL Pathway system, all welfare benefits will be distributed electronically by the year 2000. Benefit recipients will be issued with swipe cards (magnetic stripe cards that are literally 'swiped' through a card reader) in Post Offices, connected to a central computer that will advise how much money is due to be paid out. Test questions, such as asking the person's mother's maiden name, will reduce the potential for thieves to cash someone else's benefit payment. It is expected to save hundreds of millions of pounds in fraud and error.

In Spain and Portugal, smart cards are issued to people to claim unemployment benefit at kiosks, and to check on job vacancies and training opportunities. Singapore is issuing smart cards to all its three million citizens, for them to use for all their communication with the government. This works through a network of kiosks, to which the government has access, but which are provided by the private sector and used for communication with banks and other commercial organisations. Germany, too, is issuing smart cards to all its people for claims on their state health insurance.

As smart cards become more widely issued, we will begin to see the evolution of a single global health insurance scheme, probably led by the private sector. Cards would contain a person's medical record, including, for instance, images of past X-rays as well as a history of illnesses and drug treatment. The cards would also contain a record of insurance contributions, indicating what private or public health treatment the holder is eligible for. The European Commission has predicted that a Europe-wide health care system, using smart cards, will emerge at the beginning of the new century, but be led by and based on private sector provision.

The process of creating a 'self-service' welfare state is expected to achieve major savings, probably in the region of 10 per cent, but possibly as much as 20 per cent of current administrative overheads. This, along with other new technology efficiency savings, forms the basis of much of the expenditure programmes outlined by the major political parties, which are predicated on big reductions in the cost of running the state system. Nonetheless, there has been enormous reluctance by the parties to discuss this, firstly because of fear of an adverse public reaction, but also owing to the complexities of the changes and the difficulties involved in explaining them.

Nowhere is this better exemplified than in the question of fraud detection. In the early part of 1997, the Conservative government steered through Parliament the Social Security Administration (Fraud) Act, with almost no attention being paid to it by the media or public. Yet it is legislation that is of enormous significance.

Prior to this, it had been illegal for the state to undertake what is called 'data-matching' exercises – the comparison of differently compiled databases. It had, for example, been illegal for the Inland Revenue's database of tax payers to be compared with the Department of Social Security's database of benefits claimants. Because of the income tax privacy legalisation, people who were claiming benefit while working could not be detected from the Government's own databases.

This was changed by the 1997 Act, and a limited amount of data-matching was subsequently permitted, subject to a new code of practice drawn up by government departments together with the Data Protection Registrar, and overseen by the registrar. Information held by other government departments may still only be used in relation to their own functions, preventing the creation of a massive single database of citizens' information, or general data-matching.

THE WELFARE STATE

Some commentators have spoken of billions of pounds of welfare benefits fraud taking place and argued that data-matching would achieve major expenditure reductions. Estimates of achievable savings have varied between the DSS's own figures of £3bn, and £20bn suggested by the right-wing think-tank, the Adam Smith Institute. The Data Protection Registrar says that, based on the experience in Australia, which also undertook an exercise of data-matching social security and income tax records, any savings and fraud reduction will be at the lower end of the estimates.

Bids to run the Department of Social Security computer system have, though, assumed significant potential for fraud reduction, particularly if data-matching with some private sector records is also permitted. An ICL-led bid for the DSS IT administrative infrastructure involves as a partner, Experian, the credit reference agency previously known as CCN. The proposal suggests that mutual benefits can be achieved from a flow of information between the public and private sectors.

Credit references could clearly be affected by knowledge of a person's state benefits claims experience. A person who regularly claimed benefits would be a poor credit risk. Equally, someone whose credit reference status was very good would justify close examination if they claimed for a means-tested benefit.

The ICL and competing bids offer to design and implement new information systems, including all computer hardware and software, free of initial charge. They will achieve major savings, both by bringing about staffing reductions of up to 17,000 existing employees, while also cutting both fraud and manual error. Earnings for the private sector contractor will be achieved by taking a commission from the savings generated by the new system.

We can also expect that detection of some organised crime will be improved. This would be even more true if computerised records also included access to the registry of births and deaths. At present, many fraudulent claims for housing benefit and student grants are based on birth details of people who died years ago. Frank Field, the social security minister, has claimed that there is an enormous disparity between the number of national insurance numbers issued and the number of people who have worked, suggesting that phantom identities are used as the basis for widespread fraud.

Computers have already been used to track organised benefits fraud. District Audit, the arms-length agency attached to the Audit Commission, which is responsible for auditing most local authorities and health trusts, has established a cross-London computer network, incorporating all councils and Post Office branches. This has been particularly effective against gangs of fraudulent benefit claimants, and has found that, contrary to public perception, the majority of benefits fraud is conducted by landlords. Remarkably, the Audit Commission has found that each £1 spent on local government data-matching has netted a saving of £100 in fraud detection and prevention.

ARTIFICIAL INTELLIGENCE

Further savings will be achieved as the computer systems adopt 'artificial intelligence' or AI. The ability of computers to be used to aid human decision making will greatly increase as AI becomes more generally adopted. AI will be used for a wide range of applications in future years, not just to analyse government and commercial transactions to pinpoint fraud, but also to help organisations decide where to site their buildings, and to assist a variety of management decisions.

The big accountancy firms are using AI in their forensic auditing divisions. AI software can, given access to records across the relevant banks, track incoming and outgoing money, and produce a graph

THE WELFARE STATE

indicating how money was laundered, and where it finally went.

Another form of AI was used by a major telecommunications supplier to chase unpaid bills. AI software found that many subscribers failed to pay their bills, and then resubscribed with minor changes to names or addresses. The AI recognised that the slight changes masked the same identity.

There is no single system of artificial intelligence: it is a generic term for a range of different software processes that analyse what is happening and why, often replicating the way the human mind thinks, but doing complex tasks better than we could.

Neural networking is the most commonly used form of AI currently in use. The software examines past events to correlate which factors led to what outcomes, and what weight to place on each factor. In doing this it is behaving more rationally, and more calculatedly, than we could, and it can, if necessary, sift through thousands of pieces of information simultaneously.

If a neural network examines past instances of detected fraud, it can chart what symptoms most commonly cropped up. It can then go through a database of benefits claimants and produce a list of existing recipients to say which most nearly match the indicators of past fraud. Inspectors can then be allocated to those claimants to do more in-depth investigation.

The major problem with neural networks, though, is that while they can show indicators of wrongdoing, they cannot prove that anything is wrong, or explain why something is wrong. Conclusions can be produced, but they cannot be justified in a way that is acceptable to a court of law.

To do this another form of AI, the genetic algorithm, is only slightly more useful. Genetic algorithms are supposed to behave like genes – explanations of behaviour that are most nearly correct survive and mutate in an attempt to provide an even more accurate explanation.

Those explanations that are inaccurate die out, in a computerised version of Darwin's theory of evolution.

After a genetic algorithm programme is run, it can produce an explanation of what has happened, and why. Once set to run, it is immune from human interference, and cannot easily be tampered with by fraudsters trying to hide their guilt. It is an incredibly accurate system, and one that can greatly raise our understanding of the modern world. Alas, its independence is so great that it can be impossible to understand *how* it reached its conclusions, and it is, like neural networking, of limited use in courts of law. As one commentator said, hoping to get juries that understand neural networks and genetic algorithms is likely to be optimistic.

The third common form of AI is at least more intelligible. 'Fuzzy logic' examines the short-cuts the human mind takes, and follows them. It is an attempt to plug the mistakes that machines make that we would not. Given a list of names that are identical, bar an extra full stop here, an initial there, or a 'j' against a 'y' in the middle, most of us will spot the similarity. Computers will probably only notice the difference.

Fuzzy logic can put this right, and in the process notice that the Mike Smith of 7a Lucas Street who is claiming housing benefit is suspiciously similar to the Mike Smyth of Flat 1, 7 Lucas Street, and should therefore be investigated.

INTEGRATING SERVICES

If the state is to introduce this range of new means of catching fraudsters, it will also need to improve its basic services, persuading voters that the advantages flow both ways. A core element of this is the need to have an integrated communication system with the citizen.

One of the great irritants of life is the need to repeat information to

THE WELFARE STATE

different arms of the state. Why, for instance, should a woman have to apply separately for maternity benefit and for housing benefit, when both applications derive from losing income because of pregnancy?

Is it sensible that a planning application for a home improvement is handled in a different process from the request for that same local authority to give building regulations approval for that work to be carried out? If a person falls ill with a stress related ailment after being made unemployed, is it helpful for them alternately to make claims for sickness and unemployment benefit, with a further claim for income support when they run out of money?

In other words, there will have to be a pay-off for the citizen from the savings that the state will make from electronic systems. The new systems will have to offer a one-stop shop as an interface with all aspects of government.

Citizens should not be expected to know that if they go to a shop and trip over a loose floor board while buying an underweight bag of over-ripe tomatoes and want to complain, that they should go to the Health and Safety Executive quango about the accident; the county council's trading standards office about the underselling; and the district council (where one exists) about the food being off.

Integrating the central and local state into a single electronic access point creates significant political and cultural difficulties, but it will have to be done. It will require more compatibility of systems, more communication, and it may even need a re-structuring of some service responsibilities, but no one can sensibly deny that rationalisation is necessary.

Integrated electronic service centres are possible. In Cambridge, the local MP, Anne Campbell, brought together Andersen Consulting, the local authorities, the Job Centre, the Department of Education and Employment, employers, the Training and Enterprise Council, colleges, schools and children's nurseries. The result was a network of kiosks in libraries that allowed women who wanted to return to work to go to a single access point and arrange everything that they needed to sort out, from training to benefits to child care.

In Berkeley, California, an interactive community TV station has been established, which is proving very popular promoting the social welfare of the local elderly because it brings together a whole range of public information sources, together with commercial services offered by the private sector.

Pilot schemes indicate that people do not object to doing the work that the state's assistants and clerks used to do. But they very strongly want something in return. They want a break-up of the Kafkaesque state, the Soviet-type bureaucracy that still prevails in many local authorities and government departments.

What people demand is a simple system, giving them all the information they need, all sited in one place where they can easily get it. That, with our sophisticated electronic systems, we can provide if we are committed to doing so.

7 Learning

2008

Sophie, Phil's eldest daughter, would soon be 15. It was an important time as she was making decisions about which examinations to take, and which subjects to specialise in. They were decisions that would influence her university studies, and her eventual career.

Like most of her class mates, Sophie spent a lot of time researching on the World Wide Web, but it was during the process of picking her examination choices that the Web was really handy.

Sophie visited the Web sites of all the big employment agencies to see which professions were currently in the greatest demand, and what the average salary was – she was pleased to see that more pharmaceutical research scientists were needed. The sites also gave the typical identification profile of people working in this profession: their interests and their degree qualifications.

She then went to the sites of the universities offering appropriate degree courses, to see what examination passes she would need when leaving school to be accepted for those courses.

Sophie next called up the Web sites of some of the big companies which employed pharmaceutical research scientists, visiting the Web pages for careers guidance. These set out what they were looking for from graduates. There were several video presentations that claimed to represent a typical day in the life of an employee in a range of professions. Sophie found four companies whose presentations she liked, and registered with them asking if she could visit the company and be

GOVERNMENT IN THE DIGITAL AGE

shown round a laboratory.

In this way, the potential employer and the student met at an early stage. The company was able to influence the career planning of the student. In turn, the student knew what she had to achieve in order to get a job with the company.

Sophie showed the results of her research to her careers guidance teacher, who was happy with what Sophie had done.

The role of school teachers had changed significantly over the preceding five years. Pupils were left mostly to get on with things for themselves. There were far fewer teachers now, they were there mostly for support, guidance and to keep discipline. Much of the actual teaching, and the marking in some subjects, was done by computer.

By the year 2000, there was a computer on every desk of every student in every school and college. It was not a day too soon. From that point on, the nature of learning had changed completely.

Pupils had to respond continually and were more in control of their learning. All children of secondary school age were given electronic vouchers, and they could choose to spend them on whichever video lectures they wanted to call up. Some children chose the videos with their favourite presenters; others chose according to their preferred interests.

They could only choose the videos that were approved as part of their courses, but that still left enormous scope for the children's own choice. After every 10 to 15 minutes – it varied according to the subject matter, and the child's own recorded attention span – children had to answer a series of questions about the subject matter of the lecture. They could also ask their own questions, requesting further information. This greatly improved the attention span of the children, though teachers remained on hand to deal with children who got bored, mischievous or too confused.

At the end of each term, and then again at the end of each year, a computer-generated examination, unique to each pupil, quizzed children to see if they could remember what they had learnt, based on the video and classroom presentations they had actually experienced. The examination certificates were very detailed, indicating in precise terms what the children had specialised in, and what they had learnt. This level of detail was greatly appreciated by employers.

This new system had many advantages. Children who fell ill could more easily catch up with what they missed. They could even, if appropriate, do some classes from home. If they wanted, they could stay late or arrive early and do extra electronic lessons under supervision – which was very helpful for working parents. Children could even enrol for 'flexible schooling', on the same principle of flexitime hours at work.

While it reduced the numbers of teachers involved in class-based teaching, it also freed specialist teachers to be more involved in one-to-one teaching. In science, teachers could help pupils with individual research in the laboratory before they went back to their computers to write-up their personal research experience.

Children became more mature and responsible much earlier in their schooling. Of course, video presentations did not replace the traditional class room altogether. For some subjects a group discussion was important. This was true with drama, literature and with morality. But it was recognised that with subjects such as mathematics there was seldom any benefit from class room teaching – it was almost all done using the computer. Teachers were there to discuss pupils' progress, and to suggest improvements in planning learning programmes.

Sometimes, the classes could even be 'virtual classes'. Where it was important that class discussions involved children with equal and similar development, these could be convened between children anywhere in the world. This had many beneficial applications.

Children in rural Cumbria no longer had to travel 20 miles to go to school. They could learn in the reopened village school. The daughter of the British ambassador to Mongolia could live with her parents, but be schooled, virtually, with her equals in Britain. British children could participate in lessons in a school in Frankfurt, with everyone speaking German. International pen friendships had been replaced with video friendships, with the children alternating between their two languages.

The quality of schooling for children with special needs had improved tremendously. This was true not only for those with learning disabilities, who still needed far more personal support from teachers than did most children, but also for those who were extremely bright, who found the new environment much more challenging.

There was also a change to the physical environment. The big old secondary schools were now being phased out, replaced by smaller neighbourhood schools. There *was less of a problem about taking children long distances to school, achieving important reductions in vehicle emissions and road accidents. It also reduced the level of adolescent crime. With smaller schools, there were fewer big gangs around.*

A paradox of the global communications systems was that people, from their childhood on, were much more firmly rooted in their own neighbourhoods.

▲ ▲ ▲

LEARNING NOT TEACHING

TEACHING will be replaced by learning in the new educational environment. The onus will be on individuals to plan their own learning plan, which will be much more efficiently organised using ICT.

This should dramatically improve the rate at which transmitted information is absorbed, giving students the final decision on what they study, and making the learning process more interactive, allowing personal questions and answers, and incorporating instant testing to ensure that information has been absorbed.

Research has shown that students retain 80 per cent of information that have learned while 'doing', rather than just five to 10 per cent where they have read or heard it.

The new learning process will be much more tailored to the individual's own level of knowledge and ability, and students will be able to choose the style of lecturing they are most comfortable with.

There is also a growing consensus that our society must depart from the concept that education finishes when we leave school, college or university. Instead, we need 'lifelong learning', where we slip into and out of study and training as and when we and our employers want. Much of that learning will be based inside the home, using interactive TV.

But most of the TV use of the future is likely to be on a 'pay-per-

LEARNING

view' basis, charged through smart card readers attached to the TV set, and this form of learning could be expensive. It is possible, therefore, that study will be connected to a form of electronic voucher.

For the last 15 years, the right-wing political think-tanks have argued that to facilitate consumer choice in the education sector, parents should be issued with vouchers. This would allow parents to use vouchers as a contribution towards their children's education, whether it is within the private, grant-maintained, or state sectors.

Some of these think-tanks openly say that it is part of a process towards the privatisation of the education system, and the requirement for parents to make a financial top-up contribution towards their children's school fees. This is what happened for nurseries – where vouchers were introduced by the 1992-97 Conservative government – and it has been discussed in relation to the higher education sector.

If we are to have a learning-based education system, with students of all ages choosing their own resource materials, then it becomes increasingly logical to organise this through a form of voucher, issued not just to children but to adults as well. These would be credited electronically through an individual's smart card, and payment debited electronically when a video or CD was viewed. Employers might supplement the Government's learning vouchers for their own approved learning programmes.

For the learning revolution to be achieved, it will be necessary to implement a massive investment programme within our schools. This will require the purchase of individual PCs (or the new network computers, like a PC but with little or no hard disk memory), to be replaced by interactive TVs as they become state-of-the-art. These will need schools to be connected via Internet service providers, specialist education intranets and video-conference links, using high speed ISDN or ATM connections. Programmes such as these are already underway in many of our competitor nations, such as the United States, Germany,

Indonesia and Malaysia.

Once this investment has taken place, schools' role as community centres may be reinforced, with schools being used in the evenings and at weekends as virtual libraries as well as adult education centres. With a likely shift from the large urban school to the smaller village or neighbourhood school, these community centres can double as electronic village halls (see chapter two).

Pilot schemes across Europe give clear signals about how our learning programmes of the future will operate. On the west coast of Scotland, in its highlands and islands, and in rural Wales, there are many isolated communities with too few children to provide schools with traditional age and streamed classes. But they are too distant from major urban areas for each child to be sent to a larger school.

The solution has been to organise 'virtual classes', where isolated children are brought together through tele-schooling. Children have a PC each, complete with video-conference cameras and microphones, and the schools are connected by high quality ISDN cable lines. While the children will have lessons within their local schools for some subjects, for others they are brought together with their peers in other isolated communities by video-conference link, to be taught by specialist teachers who can be based dozens of miles away.

Children also gain social benefits. Instead of being isolated from children of their own ages and outlook, they can join bulletin boards and e-mail discussion groups to form new friendships, and they can do group work via video-conference links for special projects with other children of their own age.

Japanese educational centres have bought advanced virtual reality equipment from a British firm, so that children can learn about the environment through 'virtual field trips'. Using virtual reality helmets, children can 'collect' specimens and 'photograph' animals while they visit jungles, mountain ranges and remote tropical islands.

LEARNING

The changes brought about by digital technology will be as far reaching in the higher education sector as in schools. The Catalan University in Barcelona has established a 'virtual campus', to allow part-time and distance students to operate at minimum disadvantage compared with those who are present full time. Britain's Open University is increasingly gearing itself to using ICT in its relations with students.

There are specific benefits that the Department of Education and Employment has considered for Muslim girls. There are now one million Muslims in Britain, making Islam the second largest organised religion in the country. While many Muslims take a Western view on the education of girls, and on the role of women in society, in some families the girls are not permitted to mix with boys beyond infant school.

Muslim girls may be placed within state single sex schools, where these exist, but in many places there are shortages of all-girls schools, forcing the girls into madrassas – schools attached to mosques. Some of these offer effective education, but others do not, ensuring that some girls are deprived of any formal education from the time they enter their teens.

Distance learning through electronic terminals, based in the home, college, mosque or madrassa, can greatly improve the quality of schooling for Muslim girls, and of some training for Muslim women, while allowing them no contact with men outside their immediate families.

A European Commission project, Periphera, is using electronic technology to improve the education and training of a wide range of people who are marginalised from the main workforce, training them to make use of teleworking (distance working, using telecommunications technologies). One of Periphera's schemes, run by Nottingham University and a training partner, the NewLink Project, leads, at its conclusion, into membership of a co-operative business to market the participants' skills in data processing at competitive rates of pay.

In the Netherlands, a Periphera scheme is developing video-telephony for deaf people, and raising the skill levels of deaf participants to improve their employment opportunities, often through teleworking from home. Other parts of the Periphera project are assisting people in rural areas and members of ethnic minorities to gain work by training people to telework.

The European Commission itself recognises, though, that these projects will not be wholly typical of developments to come. Pilot schemes have been led by institutions – in a few years' time learning will be led by demand from the individual, from secondary school onwards.

THE RISK OF GREATER ALIENATION

Yet we must also recognise the risks of moving to a learning process. Alienation has arguably been Britain's most severe problem of the late 20th century, with millions of people out of work for long periods of time, unable to share in the rewards of a society which as a whole has earned more. Many teenagers of the early 1980s have never had a proper job in their lives, and the prospects for their happy integration into society are now slim.

As children of these earlier generations of the lost and rejected themselves reach maturity, that social alienation may multiply. Youths who see their parent's lives wasted may see little point in study. If they are to be the drivers of their own schooling they may simply reject the whole concept of study.

Technology gives us the means for overcoming this problem, but it does not guarantee that we will be successful in doing so. Unless children can be persuaded that study is enjoyable and worthwhile in its own right, and enhances their prospects for future employment, then we will simply cement the problem of society's underclass.

There is also the inheritance of a serious under-funding in our schooling and adult education, which has led to a dangerous under-use

LEARNING

of new technology. Some children have left school hardly having used a computer – at least within school – when they need to be experts if they are to obtain places within the working world, and if the country is to be able to compete with emerging nations that have invested far more heavily in new technology in schools.

Philip Crawford, managing director of Oracle UK was speaking for the whole ICT industry in Britain when he said: "Teaching a student how to access information using IT is as fundamental as learning how to read. In employment terms, if you do not have IT skills you will not be able to do many jobs."

Mr Crawford launched the manifesto for action of the Computing Services and Software Association, which called for a major training programme for Britain's teachers; targets for new technology training for every child, student and adult; and a commitment that at least one per cent of the country's education budget should be set aside for IT-based learning. It also wanted to see a research forum establish to allow industry and academia to exchange ideas, and share the results of research.

The CSSA's view was confirmed by a report from the Engineering Council, representing the sector's major corporations, and conducted by the respected Brunel University. This concluded that new technology teaching in secondary schools has been 'bedeviled by under-funding', and that investment in it must nearly double. The schools' inspectorate, Ofsted, reported in 1996 that one-third of schools was not delivering the national curriculum in IT, resulting from old equipment and poorly trained teachers.

It is clear that the Government must find the money to create a new culture in our schools, with children having ready access to modern technology, backed by the expertise of well-trained teachers and technicians. That commitment was made several years ago in the fastest developing Pacific Rim countries, such as Malaysia, Singapore and South Korea, and also in India and Pakistan.

The results of that commitment, combined with policies that are attractive to inward investors, has been that major multinational corporations have established divisions in the Far East. India and Pakistan, where high skill levels are combined with comparatively low wages, have become leading players in the computer programming sector, with their own countries' companies expanding into world markets.

Britain will not want to compete with the Far East by undercutting wages, but it must provide a labour market at least as well skilled as that in the Far East. We remain an affluent nation, and a reasonable proportion of that wealth must be invested in the current working generation and in our children if we are not to sink behind in the world table.

The alternative is that we will be condemned to become an economy without relevant skills, forced into accepting the low wages we want to avoid, offering the menial services that the tiger economies are not interested in competing for. It is not a vision of the future that many will find attractive.

(For a fuller discussion of the impact of digital technology on education please refer to the separate book in this series, *Education in the Digital Age.***)**

8 Information

2008

Phil sat on the sofa next to his interactive TV's control board, inserted his smart card into it, and dialled up his Internet server. The TV flickered, asked him his access codes, and then Phil was into the Web system. He had been to look at a house in South London, and was interested in putting in a bid to buy the property, but first he wanted some more information.

Phil entered the address of the property to find out what was on the Web pages. The Web site of the London borough of Sutton came up, which turned out to be the local authority that covered the area. He was able to find out from there the amount of council tax for the property, and the council's approximate valuation of the house; the council also gave details of the planning permission that had been granted on the house – it had approval for putting an extra room in the loft space, confirming what the sellers had said. The council's Web site also pointed out that the address was half a mile from a proposed new supermarket, and under a flight path for Heathrow.

Sutton's local plan for the area reassured Phil that there were no other major developments likely to be agreed in the next few years that would affect the property. Phil could have found out almost anything he wanted to know about Sutton council – there were thousands of Web pages of information about it. Although Phil was keener to find out more about the property he did print-out a guide to facilities in the half-mile vicinity of the house.

Next, he told the Web browser to find the street's geological survey site, which cost him 10 Euros to access, deducted from the electronic purse element of his smart card.

GOVERNMENT IN THE DIGITAL AGE

Phil learnt that five houses in the road had suffered from subsidence in the last 10 years, mostly at the other end of the street. The geological survey did point out, though, that one of the trees near to the house he was interested in had very long roots which came under the property, and that this might cause future problems. Another Web site, run by some insurance companies, told Phil about the level of burglaries in the area.

Phil printed out a copy of the report, to show his partner Bridget when she came home from work. He also checked that the Browns had legal title to the house, which they did. Phil then visited the Ordnance Survey Web site, which, on payment of another fee to be deducted from his electronic purse, then displayed a map of the street, and its immediate surroundings. He stored the 3D map as a visual display in the interactive TV's computer memory, and printed out a copy of the simple map of the area.

The local schools were a concern for Phil and Bridget. Phil visited the Web sites of the nearby primary and secondary schools, and the nearest college, and was pleased to see that several of them performed well in the league tables, yet were not oversubscribed – so their daughters would be able to get in even if they moved mid-term. Phil was conducted round on a virtual tour of the school, and saw that the equipment was modern, the classes were smart, and that the quality of drama productions and sports activities was very good.

Phil now felt as if he knew far more about the area he might move to, all from the comfort of his own home. He reflected that 10 years before he could have spent all day walking between the council offices and the library that used to be open, and still not have found out half the information.

▲ ▲ ▲

DO LIBRARIES HAVE A FUTURE?

THE next few years could see a crisis develop for the library services. As more information records become digitised, and as access to them is more commonly conducted from the comfort of the home or office, the need for local reference libraries may be less.

INFORMATION

The future may be for the virtual library, rather than the real one. This can be over-stressed, though, as people will probably want to continue to borrow from libraries books to read for pleasure. But for people who can use electronic terminals, the range of accessible databases will be so great that the traditional reference library could soon become irrelevant.

It is a trend we are beginning to see. Back copies of newspapers and magazines are today as likely to be accessed by CD-Rom or through an on-line library as they are by leafing through back-copies in reference libraries. Finding the right entry takes just a fraction of the time. Many old records, such as in the Public Records Office, are now on microfiche.

Croydon library in south London has 40 terminals for hire, allowing users to scan many thousands of databases, greatly increasing the efficiency of student research. Many residents and businesses obtain information, not in person, but by sending an e-mail request, with the answer provided by the following morning.

Whether this is the future for the reference library, or just an interim stage in its route to extinction, depends on what facilities people have in the home, and what businesses have in the office. If, as seems likely, we move towards the easy calling up of a vast range of databases through membership of closed intranets and through Web sites, then the main function of reference libraries will be more efficiently conducted on-line. There are social benefits attached to reference libraries, assisting people to understand how to obtain information and providing somewhere warm and sociable to while away time during the day, but these services might be offered in other environments.

One way forward for reference libraries is for them to abandon their general remit, recognising that few people in the future will want to walk into them to do desk-based research. Instead, if one European Commission pilot project is a guide, we will see a virtual network of

GOVERNMENT IN THE DIGITAL AGE

specialist libraries, which data exchange and inter-supply other virtual reference libraries. The EC believes that reference libraries in the future may offer services in very narrowly defined subject areas.

The European Commission is also leading a series of projects that will create a network of virtual libraries, storing digitised information from existing stores of information. At the moment it is too expensive for many organisations to scan large numbers of documents into digitised form, but scanning costs are expected to fall dramatically over the next few years, transforming access to a vast range of old reference books.

It is also possible to microfilm records, and convert those images into a digitised form which can be stored on CD-Rom or on vast computer databases. Those records can be accessed either through purchase of the CD-Rom, or through on-line interrogation of the databases.

These steps are aimed, not at getting rid of the reference library – though that may be the outcome – but at improving access to existing records. Records held across the world will be accessible from anywhere. People with disabilities, too, will have greatly improved access to reference material from their own homes. One role for the public sector may be to catalogue information sources.

If publicly-owned libraries do not respond to technology changes quickly enough, it may be the private sector, led by Internet service providers, that will increasingly operate library services on-line on a fee paying basis.

Music-on-demand and video-on-demand have been identified as prime targets for the private sector to create new markets. It is being predicted by some industry analysts that within a few years all videos and all CDs will be played not within the home, but through on-line transmission instead. If any CD or any video can be hired and played, instantly, for a minimal fee, will anyone bother to buy them any more? Similarly, will it be worth taping TV programmes or making illegal

INFORMATION

copies of CDs on cassette? If hire fees are not kept low, illicit recordings will be made. The downward pressure on CD and video prices would be enormous.

One application of the interactive TV will be a type of jukebox of every CD in the world, and of every old TV programme and film ever shown. This has profound implications not merely for the continuation of public music libraries, but also for many businesses. Video hire shops and record shops could disappear, and independent recording labels could be threatened if income from 'jukebox' plays does not match that of sales income. The music industry could be transformed from the production of CDs to the production of a single recording, stored as an audio database, available on-line.

There is the further risk that there will be a massive increase in bootleg recordings made available on-line, undermining the legitimate music industry.

The likelihood of these developments being achieved is dependent on several factors, not least the creation of an electronic payment system that is capable of charging a few pence for each piece of data transmission. These developments are well under way through the use of smart cards in particular.

Smart cards will soon transform much of our lives. We can already use them, at least in some parts of the world, for pay phone calls, for pay-per-view TV, to access our bank accounts, to receive welfare payments, as identification, and to pay for travel.

The latest generation of computers contain smart card readers, which will be as integral a part of a computer as the disk drive is now. As computers evolve into interactive TVs, they will contain cameras, microphones, fingerprint readers, making them more comprehensive communication tools, and allowing information on the smart card to be confirmed by the physical appearance of the user. This will create effective controls on access to sensitive intranet sites.

These smart cards are also the basis on which small fees can be charged. This is important for creating a market in information. Without being able to charge a few pence for information, there is no market for private sector involvement. Information is otherwise either high cost or no cost.

It also overcomes the security problems that have inhibited the development of electronic commerce. We can expect that within a few years the majority of business-to-business transactions will be conducted electronically (see chapter 10).

Creating a commercial market for the low cost transmission of CDs, videos, public documents, back copies of newspapers and magazines and pages of books, is likely to destroy much of what is today regarded as a public sector function. It may be that this market will not be controlled by individual companies, but may be operated through partnerships between Internet service providers and public bodies. It is nonetheless likely that the shape of our information services will change beyond recognition in the next few years.

THE ROLE OF THE WEB

An illustration of the likely future can be seen when we examine the Web site of Hampshire County Council. In fact, Hampshire's Web site, HantsWeb, is a public information service extracted from its intranet system, HantsNet. HantsNet primarily exists for council staff and other parts of the local public sector, as a means of increasing coordination within and between public bodies. Access is restricted through use of passwords, and the level of information available to a person depends on their personal authorisation.

Local businesses can subscribe to HantsNet, so that employees can obtain up-to-date information on road conditions and transport reports.

INFORMATION

It also gives them an easy means of looking at council committee papers, and council decisions. There are a total of 17,000 registered users of HantsNet. As well as being accessed by users through PCs, the public sections of HantsNet can also be read at kiosks in the council's libraries, museums and other public buildings.

Part of the public element of the HantsNet intranet is extracted for HantsWeb. Where HantsNet has two million pages of council information, HantsWeb has 300,000 pages, held on Hampshire County Council's host computer. The site has over half a million visits each month, and is updated daily.

HantsWeb is available to local community groups, 20,000 of which are on its Community Users Information, or Cousin, section. The site also contains an e-mail directory of all known Internet users in the county, and a business information service to encourage local firms to use the site. HantsWeb is also being made available as a Web TV service to residents in the county with cable TV connections.

Other types of specialist organisations, too, are looking to the Web. Trading standards officers, who are employed by councils, have set up their own Web site, TSNet, as a consumer advice service to the public.

Several councils have established Web sites to promote tourism and the use of local leisure sites and hotels. MISTi kiosks have been developed by ICL, in partnership with councils in West Cornwall, to create an electronic sales infrastructure, which has proved particularly popular for peripatetic tourists to book accommodation. The kiosks allow people to inspect a hotel virtually, helping them gain a clear idea about the standard of accommodation.

Local authorities in Cornwall report that the project is self-financing by promoting the area to tourists, encouraging people to visit more often and to stay longer. It has also helped to establish a system by which local businesses are encouraged to inter-trade, keeping more locally generated income in the local economy.

GOVERNMENT IN THE DIGITAL AGE

This same objective was behind a project run by North East Lincolnshire Council, as part of its strategy to support the local economy. The council wanted businesses to recognise the environmental as well as economic benefits of local inter-trade, and promoted events to help local businesses network, supporting this through an electronic bulletin board which also enabled local businesses to tender for public and private sector contracts and to ask for an interest in co-operative ventures.

The Australian government is one of the most advanced in putting its departments onto the Web. Government policy statements, press releases, legislative proposals and annual reports are entered on its Web pages as a matter of course. Development has been led by the Department of Communications and the Arts, a body which has a core responsibility for ensuring that Australia uses the most up-to-date communication technologies.

Among the projects the DCA has headed-up have been the Australian Museums On-Line service, which contains the full catalogues of many of the country's museums. The Australian Cultural Network will contain full catalogues of collections, and will hold copies of most of the country's collections on its Web pages. (Most of the world's major galleries are doing the same.) The One Stop Arts Shop is a Web site that will contain information on grants and public support programmes for the arts in Australia.

As PCs – and their successors – become better at receiving audio signals, so their use will further evolve. On one level, we will see PCs being used to make cheap phone calls, using toll free and cheap local rate connections through Internet service providers for international calls.

On another level we will find that Web sites increasingly become the repository of digitally stored audio files, that can be accessed through the latest generation of home terminals. The National Sound Archive, based in the British Library, is already creating a single collection not

INFORMATION

only of most music recordings, but also of a vast range of important speeches, radio programmes and dramatic performances.

Initially the National Sound Archive will be accessible only to visitors to it and major libraries in other European cities. Eventually, though, it could be available from home in the same way that Web sites can be accessed, so that all the world's recorded music is available on one massive jukebox. Not so coincidentally, the name of this European Commission development scheme is called Project Jukebox.

Demand for the use of these new technologies will probably be as much for the ordinary as the luxury. Land searches and planning applications are the type of day-to-day functions of local and central government that everyone expects to run efficiently, and only notices when they don't. Digital technology can make the services more user-friendly, and reduce the time it takes to use them.

The Scottish Office is creating an electronic land and property information service that could be a model for a cross-Britain system. It brings together into one network the databases and the Scottish land registry, local authority planning departments, the Ordnance Survey and Scotland's Royal Institute of Chartered Surveyors. ScotLIS will provide a one-stop-shop approach to land queries, providing information on land and property ownership, land use approval, utility service provision, road and geological surveys, and details on which properties are listed.

Applications for planning permission, objections to planning applications, land searches, assessing land for subsidence risk and proposing the listing of historic buildings will all be possible from the same public access kiosks. Conveyancing should become quicker, cheaper and more comprehensive as a result. Several English local authorities are setting up similar systems, though these may be less comprehensive initially.

Sheffield City Council has established a geographic information system (GIS) that not only makes land searches quicker, it is also the basis for the council to access all information related to particular addresses. Street furniture (such as road lighting) is listed, making the logging of faults more reliable, and it is also used to determine which children are entitled to bus passes, by computerising the calculation of how far children have to travel to school.

But the most ambitious projects aim to convert Europe's existing major urban centres into so-called 'digital cities', connected by the latest ATM (asynchronous transfer mode) technology, with a network of kiosks, and home access to public information. At the core is a host computer, run for the municipality, containing a vast array of public service information. This can include, as in the case of Manchester, links not just between local businesses, but between Manchester's Bangladeshi businesses and traders in Bangladesh.

Singapore is the most advanced exponent of this approach, and its model has been closely examined by the British government's Central Information Technology Unit (CITU). Singapore aims to have a network of 300 public access kiosks by the year 2000, which are being funded not by government, but by the private sector. CITU advisors believe that this approach should be copied in Britain (the Conservative government agreed, but Labour and the Liberal Democrats have both stated their opposition to this approach).

Public access facilities will be integrated into banks' multimedia kiosks – which will gradually replace the old cash machines, bringing together cash withdrawal and payment facilities with state-of-the-art marketing techniques, such as recorded and live video-conference links. Each time the kiosks are used for public access purposes the private sector provider of the kiosks will make a charge to the Government.

The Singapore government believes that this network of kiosks will provide a more friendly interface for its citizens, and greatly reduce the amount of correspondence and phone calls staff have to deal with. It

INFORMATION

also believes that it is appropriate that the private sector should pay for the infrastructure, and operate kiosks on the basis of previous development experience.

The question of who should manage the new infrastructure will be a key question for our politicians, and it is one on which there is no consensus. It is a question that needs careful examination.

⑨ Paying the piper

WHAT Britain needs, and what it can afford, are increasingly at odds, according to many economists and policy specialists. The core of the problem is that digital technology is driving an ever more global economy that will enable people and companies to buy products and services from wherever they can be provided cheapest.

▲ ▲ ▲

For Britain to be effective in that global economy we must compete by reducing the costs of government to the level of that of the emerging nations whose rates of taxation are below ours, according to the prevailing neo-liberal ideology that seems to be accepted by all the main parties in all the major countries. This drove Conservative governments in the 1980s and 1990s to try to bring the UK's public expenditure below 40 per cent of gross domestic product.

Digital technology offers both an opportunity and a threat in this drive towards reduced public expenditure. The opportunity is in the potential savings it offers through increased productivity. As we have already seen in chapter six, a welfare state system that is based on citizens inputting their own data is self-evidently cheaper than one where thousands of staff are employed to enter data .

On the pretext – sometimes actually achieved – of a more customer-friendly service, governments can persuade the population to use electronic systems to apply for benefits, and to make annual tax returns, for instance. This can improve the quality of the contact, as the electronic systems are much better than forms in guiding individuals through a bureaucratic process. If information has been left out, the electronic form cannot be submitted. The waste of days waiting for welfare benefits, because a box was inadvertently overlooked, will be a thing of the past.

In turn, governments can eliminate a whole raft of data inputting and data processing employees. As a transitional arrangement, the scanning of documents, especially where they have handwriting recognition abilities, as at the Driver and Vehicle Licensing Agency, can also achieve important savings. Computer determination of benefits applications is also more reliable, reducing the incidence of error and of fraud.

The Inland Revenue has now introduced electronic versions of self-assessment forms, allowing businesses and accountants to file annual returns by e-mail. With the banking system increasingly moving to electronic processing, and the introduction of on-line banking, it can be assumed that it will soon be possible not only to file returns electronically, but also to file payments – by issuing an electronic authorisation to a bank simultaneous with submitting a return, or else by deducting a period's tax liability from an electronic purse connected to the electronic terminal.

Kenneth Clarke, the former Chancellor of the Exchequer, claimed that extending the computerisation of government could achieve savings in the administration of government of around 12 per cent. Advisors to government believe this may have been too pessimistic – some talk of 20–50 per cent reductions in overhead costs.

This ignores any savings that can be achieved by data matching. With computer records compared – such as those of the Inland

Revenue, the Department of Social Security and local authorities – it will be much harder to get away with various frauds, such as working while in receipt of benefit.

But these long term savings come with a short term cost. An enormous investment is required in new digital infrastructure. As local authorities have shown, capital expenditure controls sit badly alongside attempts to modernise computer systems. Some councils have made bad purchasing decisions, saddling themselves with systems that were out-of-date when bought, but are too expensive to be replaced for the foreseeable future.

Even spread over a number of years, the servicing of capital debt for new computer infrastructure is an expensive business. With the rate of change in state-of-the-art technology, and the risk of getting it wrong, it becomes prohibitively so.

There is also the problem of down-time, and the question of optimum unit size. A typical public sector computer system only runs during the working day, leaving it unused for two thirds of the time. Private sector contractors can achieve operational savings by running public sector functions alongside other applications, making better use of expensive central equipment. By operating parallel computers, some linked across the world, they are shielded against the problems of system and power failures, avoiding problems with data retrieval during and after breakdowns.

There is a very strong case for public sector organisations contracting-out the running of their computer facilities. Public bodies often pay uncompetitive salaries to senior staff, particularly in the computing field, and their choice of equipment is sometimes in error as a result.

Contracting-out can make efficiency gains, which reduces the cost of an IT function. It can also lead to deferment of payment, by contracting for payment by result. It might be thought that as

PAYING THE PIPER

government, including local government and NHS trusts, can borrow money more cheaply than the private sector, that it should be able to finance IT infrastructure more cheaply than business can.

However, there is the problem of capital expenditure restraints, and the fact that the speed of change of digital technology means that it is now normal for systems to need replacing within a few years of purchase, in order to take advantage of the latest efficiency saving equipment. In practice, for a public body this would mean that technology is likely to need replacing before it has been paid for. Clearly paying the debt charges simultaneously for several generations of equipment is absurd.

What is more sensible is to pass the risk of technology obsolescence onto the private sector, building into the contract a factor for sharing savings achieved by improving operational systems. In this way there is a motivation for the two parties to work together in a spirit of partnership, while there will also be incentives for the contractor to upgrade equipment sooner rather than later.

By spreading overheads across several customers, a private sector contractor can finance the regular updating of systems which a public body would find impractical.

It is now legitimate to ask whether the role of government includes supplying a modern ICT infrastructure, or merely to ensure that it is supplied, and is accessible to all. Rob Wirszycz, director general of the ICT representative body in the UK, the Computing Services and Software Association, has argued: "We think the role of government is to facilitate this, in the context of an overall vision. We don't believe government should be involved in technology because technology is not government's role."

There is specifically the question of financing multimedia kiosks. Kiosks cost between £3,000 and £15,000 each, depending on the level of sophistication, but with transaction and maintenance costs on top.

Basic touch screen terminals have much greater limitations, often limited to providing passive information. As kiosks become more common, they will also offer more complexity in operation, linked to microphones, speakers and cameras to facilitate video-conference links, scanners for document sharing, keyboards for complex instruction issuing and question answering and smart card readers to personalise the interaction.

The level of sophistication of future kiosks can be judged already. At some Japanese workplaces, NCR has installed kiosks that allow users to order a comprehensive shopping list, either for delivery to home at a set time, or for collection at a shop later in the day. We are increasingly likely to see specially adapted kiosks used in a workplace setting.

At the core of kiosk development is the question of whether we shall see separate terminals for public and private sector functions. British Telecom has used ICL's expertise to install kiosks across much of London, which may indicate how phone boxes will evolve. The primary function of these kiosks is to service commercial organisations that pay a commission to BT per transaction. Users include hotels, theatres and other leisure activities. Yet there is also a public information aspect to BT's kiosks, providing maps and helplines as well as publicising local authority activities.

Singapore is creating a network of 300 kiosks across the city. Although the Singapore government will provide public information services, including full electronic access to all parts of government, these kiosks are financed and managed by the private sector. They are operated by a joint venture called 'Nets', owned by seven Singapore banks, that is also responsible for the country's Eftpos (electronic funds transfer at point-of-sale) system, and is developing a local electronic purse.

The Singapore government will pay Nets for each transaction on the kiosk. Eventually the kiosks will be both a means of conducting a range of financial transactions, including cash withdrawals, payments, transfers and purchasing financial products such as pensions and mortgages, and a one-stop-shop for all government services. Their first application was to sell tickets for a range of leisure activities, including plays and cinemas. Some cash machines in South Africa also sell film tickets.

In the early 1990s the British government saw Singapore's experience as the best model for its own roll-out of multimedia kiosks. Former information technology minister Ian Taylor even went so far as to say that he expected future elections and referenda to be conducted on kiosks owned and managed by the private sector, many of which would be sited within banks and building societies. Government advisors in the Central Information Technology Unit, CITU, were strongly in favour of this approach.

Philip Crawford, managing director of Oracle UK, has argued that this approach is justified not merely on cost grounds, but on grounds of convenience as well. It has to be recognised, he believes, that patterns of individual behaviour may no longer take people into public buildings. "(Kiosks) should be in libraries, government buildings, higher education colleges. But there is no reason why they could not be made available in shops and banks – the places where people go."

The Labour Party in opposition, however, took the view that it is important to have separate public and private sector kiosks. At the same time, Labour argued that public access kiosks should not be a cost to the taxpayer.

One way of achieving this is to encourage commercial sponsorship of specific-function kiosks, to avoid cost obligations falling on the public sector. An example of this would be kiosks for renewing driver and vehicle licences, that might be financed by a motor insurance company. The pay-off for the insurer would be logos on the terminal, prominent commercial identification on the screen layout, and a default setting that returned the screen to offer that insurer's policies, possibly complete with an automatic print-out quote for the user's vehicle.

David Denison, local government consultant with ICL, explained a type of arrangement his company was interested in. "One option is that the private sector provides the kiosk, and runs it, but bolts a local authority's name on the front to attract users, while providing both public and private sector information."

There may be problems with these approaches. Tying a commercial organisation so closely to specific public services may give the impression of official sanction or support for the business. Whether this impression is acceptable is clearly a policy decision. An opposing argument will be that the same concern could arise at the use of any privately owned kiosk used for public service access, but the relationship in the case of sponsorship may appear more intimate, and more of a product recommendation.

However, there seems little resistance to the principle that it is commerce that will be paying for our new electronic infrastructure. In the candid words of a European Commission document: "Financing the information society is a task for the private sector."

All the main parties in British politics now believe in attracting private money for public works, whether it is called the private finance initiative by the Conservatives, or public and private partnerships, as new Labour more often calls it.

It is equally true that it is the private sector that will have to pay for the 'superhighway' infrastructure, cabling up the whole country with high quality ISDN and ATM links. In opposition new Labour obtained the agreement of BT to connect all schools with ISDN links for free, in return for lifting the controls on BT supplying video-on-demand and other TV entertainment services. Since then, the cable companies have also offered to connect many schools.

Unfortunately, this does not resolve the whole problem about a national infrastructure. Rural areas, although assumed to be wealthy, contain many pockets of severe poverty. Without ISDN cable connections the aim of promoting teleworking in rural areas will not be feasible. One option is tighter regulatory controls on the telecommunications and television industry, which could require operators to provide high quality cable links in rural areas.

However, there are people who believe that this problem can be overcome by developments in satellite and radio-wave technologies, which may actually see the cable industry redundant. Many countries have failed to invest in modern telephone systems, and there is now an urgent need to create a new telecommunications infrastructure, not only to make it compatible with computing and information technologies, but just to create a working phone system.

Many parts of the old Soviet Union still use telephone exchanges and connections that were built in the 1920s, and have barely been updated since. In Estonia there has been heavy investment by Scandinavian businesses to create a new telecommunications system based on radio-wave technology, the price of which is coming down quickly. It is also cheaper to instal than cabling up a whole country. The same approach is being adopted in South Africa.

Where Estonia uses localised radio-wave transmitters and aerial receivers, others are using satellites as transmitters. This is particularly attractive to international travellers as it may assist them to use mobile phones anywhere in the world. Radio-wave technology may be the wrong answer to the infrastructural problems, though, with some people worried about the long-term health affects.

Ionica is a Cambridge-based telecommunications company that uses radio-waves instead of land cabling. Before it was launched it commissioned a report from the National Radiological Protection Board, asking whether health problems can be caused by radio-wave signals. The report concluded that there were no grounds for concern. The European Commission is conducting further research into possible links between radio-wave telephones and illness, particularly brain tumours.

The fear is that damage may be caused to the brain when radio-waves are used for phone traffic. One theory is that the body, and the brain in particular, can act as a signal receiver, causing cell mutation, and benign or malignant tumours. It may take years to resolve whether these fears are well founded.

An alternative to radio-waves and cables is to use ordinary electricity cables for telecommunications traffic. Norweb, the north-west England electricity supplier, is conducting detailed research into the potential for using electricity cables for telephone calls. The provisional findings are that this works well, and Norweb believes that within a few years it will be reading customers' meters without having to visit properties, through distance-read facilities connected to electricity cables. Whether the same cabling can also be used to replicate the quality of ISDN connections is too early to say.

In past decades these questions would have been the responsibility of governments to resolve. Now they are firmly in the private sector's hands. There may be no choice, given the acceptance of free market principles throughout the world, but there are obvious risks attached to this approach.

One issue is that the private sector may be more willing to embrace higher risk technologies than governments would accept. Another is that whoever pays the piper calls the tune. Governments are now dependent on the private sector to provide the digital infrastructure for the new century. That must inevitably shift the balance of power between the private and public sectors. Commerce is in the driving seat.

The result of this is that equality of provision may be a thing of the past. Without strong regulation – which has a cost attached that the private sector may argue would make it internationally uncompetitive – telecoms businesses may not be willing to provide equal access to

PAYING THE PIPER

equal services in all parts of the country. It is just one of many new ethical challenges that governments will have to struggle with over the coming years.

10 Managing government

WHAT is government? Any answer is different today to what it would have been 10 years ago, and it is constantly changing.

▲ ▲ ▲

The Conservative administration claimed it had reduced the role of government as a provider to such an extent that all its remaining services could be provided electronically. That may be an exaggeration – waging wars is an obvious exception, though even that has a strong element of electronic service delivery – but it is more true than it is untrue.

Hospitals, trains, education, the payment of welfare benefits and inflation control have all to a greater or lesser extent been taken out of the direct responsibility of government, transferred into a more arms-length arrangement, or simply been privatised. What has been left, in theory at least, is the setting of policy objectives, and the overseeing of contractual arrangements with the outside bodies that must implement government policy.

The citizen can communicate directly with the delivery arm of government, to ask for service improvements, or enquire about progress on an outstanding problem. Communication with the core of government would then mostly be about improving democracy, helping politicians to be better aware of the views of constituents.

MANAGING GOVERNMENT

Theory and practice may diverge in the way the individual sees things. Executive agencies already exist to run most government services, employing the majority of civil servants, yet to the public the services remain the responsibility of the Government. Similarly, the public remains unclear which public services are carried out by local authorities, which by executive agencies, which by quangos, and which by government itself. And why should the public be expected to know?

It is essential that digital technology allows the public to communicate with the entire public sector as a one-stop service. People will react badly to the electronic continuation of old-style public service demarcation lines.

This has several repercussions. First, local and central government – and any new regional assemblies – must learn to work closely together. Second, quangos, (if they are to continue at all) must be better integrated into the business of government, and will have to be accountable to the public through electronic questioning. And thirdly the business at the heart of government will have to be re-engineered.

Corporations have been radically reformed over the last 15 years or so. Objectives have been re-assessed, hierarchies slimmed down, divisional responsibilities reviewed, organisations reduced to core activities, and extraneous tasks contracted-out. The public sector has not been immune to this process, and the administrative base of many public bodies has been cut back under the pressure of expenditure controls. Yet many public bodies are much less changed than their commercial counterparts.

Public organisations ranging from civil service departments, to police forces, to local authorities, are still based on a 1920s approach which modelled them on the armed services. They remain extremely hierarchical, with fewer managerial layers removed than has been achieved in commerce and industry. Public services still have stark demarcation lines between departments and organisations, even when responsibilities naturally overlap between them. Senior managers are often ICT-illiterate, not even using e-mail – whereas comparable managers in the private sector are fully abreast of new technology as part of their daily working routines.

In the commercial world there is a move towards joint ventures, with partnerships formed between companies that are fierce rivals in other respects. Examples of this approach can be seen in tendering for government contracts. In one tender you will see ICL and Andersen working together for an ICT contract. In another you will see them in conflict, operating with other partners. In retail banking, the Royal Bank of Scotland not only operates its own banking service, but also operates in partnership with Tesco, providing the supermarket chain's banking service.

Yet in the public sector it is the rivalry and refusal to work in partnership that is more obvious, even though objectives are theoretically shared. An example is the administration of housing benefit.

Housing benefit has been administered for many years by local authorities – sometimes incompetently. It is the Department of the Environment that oversees the councils' administration of the benefit, and which has failed to pull the worst councils up to decent administrative standards, or ensure that councils resource their housing benefits departments properly. An Audit Commission report a few years ago found that one council had failed to open any housing benefits correspondence for a year.

As councils' housing benefit administration got worse the housing benefit bill rose ever higher. Partially this was because councils failed to spot fraud. This in turn was because departments were badly run, under-resourced and had no incentive to find fraud – indeed they lost DoE grant when fraud was uncovered. But, worse still, it was the DoE that set some of the rules to determine when housing benefit was paid, and it was the DoE that cut subsidy for new homes that led to increased

MANAGING GOVERNMENT

housing rents. Yet it was the Department of Social Security that picked up the increasing housing benefit bill.

Common sense says that problems will arise when one department sets the rules, and another department picks up the bill. There is a lack of management and political accountability for errors in judgement, and irresponsibility is the outcome. It should have been obvious years ago that a higher degree of inter-departmental co-operation and joint responsibility was required.

Moreover, until recently, information held by housing benefit administrators on individual claimants would not normally be shared with the DSS itself, even though the DSS was paying the bill. This helped fraud to perpetuate.

This is the type of problem that has led the UK's ICT industry representative body to say that there needs to be a fundamental re-engineering of government operations. The Computing Services and Software Association argues that the present range of government departments is no longer necessarily the correct one, and that, at the very least, services need to be organised on a modular basis, centred on issues, rather than on a departmental basis.

Responsibilities are often the results of accidents of history, rather than decisions consciously taken for the sake of efficiency. Why, for instance, are some road repairs undertaken by district councils, others done by county councils, and yet others by the Highway Agency on behalf of the Department of Environment, Transport and the Regions (DETR)? Is this efficient? If there were a single body with roads responsibilities, would it be easier to co-ordinate relationships with utility companies?

Relationships with the ICT industry, too, are unhelpfully disparate. As well as the Central Information Technology Unit, reporting to the Cabinet Office, other departments involved include the Department of National Heritage, the Department for Education and Employment, and the DETR, as well as the Department of Trade and Industry where the ministers mainly responsible for ICT are based.

There is a belief within the ICT industry that it carried too little weight with the Conservative government, and that this was not merely harmful to the industry, but also prevented the Government making the most of ICT development. This is despite the considerable progress the Conservative administration did achieve, particularly under the guidance of Deputy Prime Minister Michael Heseltine.

Mr Heseltine was responsible for creating CITU to ensure that government departments' approach to new technology was integrated and co-ordinated at the policy level. Until CITU was established, it had not even been possible for civil servants to e-mail each other across departments. It was also quickly found that there had been little attempt at co-ordinating procurement, with the result that equipment varied enormously, and was often incompatible.

To give CITU the weight and intelligence it needed, it co-opted some of the most senior minds of the ICT industry, including John Elmore, technology director of ICL Services. Mr Elmore recalled: "CITU was given very loose terms of reference. We had to radically improve the delivery of services to government's customers. We had to reduce the costs of government. Third, we had to ask how do we maximise the resources we have in the public and private sectors to meet these first two factors? These resources were not just of money, but of information as well."

RE-ENGINEERING GOVERNMENT

The arguments presented to the Government by CITU and by the industry through its representative body the CSSA, led to consideration of how public services can be provided on a more episodic basis, rather than being departmentally based. Those major episodes were considered to be birth, marriage, schooling, employment, retirement or redundancy, and death. A parallel series of episodes can be mapped for companies.

In the future, through the blueprint outlined by CITU, a pregnant woman would be able to go to a kiosk, or access government services through a home or work PC, and use an integrated system to communicate with the public services in planning her pregnancy. She could apply for maternity benefit; apply for other benefits such as housing benefit, council tax benefit and income support; apply for her own maternity leave and her partner's paternity leave if they work for the public sector; register the birth; notify the birth to state bodies such as the DSS, her general practitioner, and her housing association or council landlord; and request to move to a larger council home – all through a seamless electronic process.

The ethos behind CITU's 'Government.Direct' green paper, subtitled 'a prospectus for the electronic delivery of government services', was to consult as to how to use ICT more effectively in providing government services. Those within CITU recognised – even if ministers did not publicly acknowledge this – that the outcome was likely to be a wholesale re-engineering of the structure of government.

This reflected an acknowledgement that, through the use of new technology, industry has reduced its costs of production by between 20 and 50 per cent. Yet the British government has failed to even approach these savings. A further 10 per cent cost reduction is on offer to the public sector if it can follow the lead of the financial services industry and assist its customers to do its own data inputting.

One way in which services might be geared towards episode-based services can be envisaged by examining the New Zealand public sector reforms. Where different government departments are capable of operating a related service – such as air/sea rescue, which the three armed services and the police all have the infrastructure to undertake – they tender competitively to operate the service.

GOVERNMENT IN THE DIGITAL AGE

An option for the British government is that instead of reconstructing existing departmental boundaries, they might continue to be made smaller, but be given the opportunity to tender for managing related episode-based electronic services.

Local authorities, too, have been keen to re-engineer, to make departments reflect natural boundaries more closely. Dave Denison, ICL's local government consultant, recalled: "One unitary council considered starting a children's department for education and children's social services, but it was blocked by the technology and the existing databases. IT can be a barrier to this happening, not an enabler.

"There are 450 councils all mirroring central government's approach, but all doing it differently. Local government hasn't thought about how to deliver services jointly with central government. The re-engineering of departments is easier said than done. Lots of authorities are putting an effort into making the front-end homogeneous. A lot of the management consultancy done by us has an emphasis on this rather than on IT."

Mr Denison says that three local authority functions are particularly affected by new technology – economic regeneration, lifelong learning and community information – and this fact will increasingly influence departmental structures.

One of the problems reported by Mr Denison is that after 25 years of trying there is still no systemic linkage between the local and county plans where these are the responsibility of different but parallel councils. He predicts it may be another 10 years before such harmonies exist.

"Data-matching by central government is not the same as sharing a single database. It is impractical to have the same software operating all the time. It is getting more possible using data-warehousing techniques, but most data-warehouses do data-matching rather than data-sharing," Mr Denison explained.

Despite the progress made by CITU, the ICT industry believes

MANAGING GOVERNMENT

Britain continues to lag badly behind competitor nations. An example of this is in schooling, where ICT has made only a modest impact. CSSA warns that unless schools make better use of new technology then Britain will produce a generation of people who will be under-skilled compared with competitor nations.

There is also, says the industry, a need for government to develop its role as an exemplar and influencer. Although ICT is now the world's fourth largest industry, producing some of the world's richest entrepreneurs, the UK investment sector has put only six per cent of its money into ICT.

The CSSA argues that government must use its influence on banks to review the way they make investment decisions, and help the finance houses train more of their executives to understand the ICT sector better. There is now growing evidence that developing ICT companies are moving away from Britain to base themselves in the US because of the shortage of venture capital in the UK. The US is particularly attractive as a base, because its NASDAQ (North American Securities Dealers' Automated Quotations) stock exchange understands new technology much better than do British venture capitalists, and 40 per cent of NASDAQ quoted stocks are in the ICT sector.

A NEW MEDIUM FOR COMMERCE

Malaysia's government has gone even further, saying that the creation of an electronic infrastructure for government creates demand for new systems that will give its domestic companies a head start in international markets. This is the key reason why Malaysia tenders its contracts through electronic systems.

In any case it is not a decision that is hard to justify. Electronic commerce is 90 per cent cheaper than traditional forms. Expert analysts believe that the Internet will, within five years, be the basis for most business-to-business trade. It makes sense for governments to adapt to this trend sooner rather than later, assisting domestic companies to recognise a new commercial imperative while taking advantage of important cost savings.

Electronic media are ideal for facilitating transactions. E-mail can instantly be sent off to any number of companies requesting tenders for contracts. Urgent supplies can be commissioned on a same-day basis, even after a comprehensive tendering exercise. Open requests for tenders, joint venture partners or capital can be posted on bulletin boards. Information is more accurately recorded than when using telephones.

The World Wide Web is also of increasing importance for commerce. Annual reports and company information are available on the Web, and several Web sites operate as shopping malls, selling groceries, CDs and books on-line.

The significance of the Web for electronic commerce will grow as 'intelligent agents' develop. Intelligent agents, which are also called 'search engines' or 'bloodhounds', are instructed to find things on the Web. They may be instructed to create a list of companies whose annual reports include an environmental audit. Or they may be told to find which retailer of CDs offers the cheapest price for a particular album. Or they may report on which construction and leisure consortia are keen to tender on a design, build, finance and operate basis for a new swimming pool.

CALL CENTRES

It is not only multimedia kiosks, interactive TVs and Web sites accessible through home and office PCs, that will be the front-ends of one-stop-shop public services. We can also expect to see a growth in the use of call centres and telephone computer integration (TCI) within the public sector.

MANAGING GOVERNMENT

There are now over 5,000 call centres in Britain, receiving telephone calls, not just from all over the country, but often from across Europe, and in some instances from the other side of the world. Creating 0800 freephone numbers, or toll free numbers as they are called elsewhere in the English-speaking world, has led to the growth of the phenomenon of centralised marketing, phone sales and customer support centres.

General Electric's financial services division, GE Capital, has its European call centre in Leeds, a city that has become one of Europe's specialist financial services centres. First Direct, the telephone bank, has two call centres to handle account queries, as has the Co-operative Bank, which is weaning its customers away from branch banking into telephone banking. ShareLink, owned by leading US share brokers Charles Schwab, operates an expanding call centre in Birmingham for phone share dealing.

In some call centres, a single phone number is used for all incoming calls. Where all staff are occupied on incoming calls overflow calls may be transferred to employees based elsewhere in the UK or even in Ireland, the United States or Australia, utilising optimum time zones.

Call centres are a development based on the reversal of the old marketing adage that 'location is everything'. Today it is almost possible to argue that location is nothing. Parking tickets issued in London are data processed in Scotland, summonses are issued from Scotland, and phone queries are handled in Scotland. This is all down to the impact of digital technology.

With the reliable and fast transference of telecommunications traffic to almost anywhere in the world, we are seeing work move to low wage areas that in the past were too remote to be taken advantage of. This means that correspondence dictated by a GP practice in Washington in the United States is sent to Bangalore in India, where it is typed and e-mailed back to the practice in just a few minutes. It also means that India has emerged as the world's leading supplier of computer software.

Several airlines, including British Airways, have transferred part of their ticketing reservations and processing operations to third world countries – mostly the Dominican Republic for US airlines, and India for European air operators. BA has followed this up with the transference of further administrative support tasks, including some of its accountancy functions.

This process will create pressure for the levelling out of wages internationally and within countries. In the short term jobs can be expected to move away from high wage countries, such as Germany, and towards lower wage economies, particularly in the Pacific Rim. Britain has benefited from this trend, with wages and labour conditions inferior in the UK to those in other North European countries.

It is also possible that language will be the most important factor in future commercial relations. Instead of the European Union becoming increasingly important to commerce, it could be the English language ties binding the Commonwealth that re-establishes it as an important trading block.

Within Britain, call centre location is tending towards those cities with high unemployment and low wages. Cities that are attracting call centre investment include Leeds, Newcastle, Birmingham, Glasgow and Belfast. This may eventually lead to the equalisation of wages across the country, though it should be noted that call centres are more likely to be sited in big cities which have good telecommunications links, including ISDN cabling.

Call centres are a central part of the digital future. In the US, three per cent of the workforce is employed in them. Almost half of all call centres in Europe are sited within Britain, not least because it is US corporations that are leading the trend towards their creation, and the common language bond makes the UK an attractive location.

One of the other trends possible with call centres is the use of caller line identification (CLI). This means that when an incoming call is received, the phone number is recognised by the computer. Phone directory and address databases are instantly interrogated, and the address of the call and names of all occupants are displayed on screen.

Any outstanding problems on the account are also retrieved from the data warehouse, and displayed. It should mean that it will be possible to route calls from nominated phone lines to specific employees – for instance, households where some residents only speak Urdu could be answered by Urdu speaking staff.

The drawback with CLI is that lots of calls are not made from home, but from work. However, many employers are finding that computer information systems give them a greater ability to monitor staff activities, which may reduce the number of personal calls made from work. The same principle with CLI can be used for managers to receive a regular print-out of staff's calls, together with the names of who they call.

The employer as 'big brother' may be further boosted if PCs are replaced in the office environment by network computers – cheaper terminals that share central databases and have limited hard disk capacity. These could report staff's activities on the terminal, in order to prevent personal Internet surfing.

It is important not to consider developments such as call centres in isolation from other trends, such as the move towards outsourcing. Call centres may not be operated by the companies they serve. Matrixx Marketing is a US corporation which operates in the UK from Newcastle, and achieves maximum efficiency by balancing demand between a range of customers, many of which are themselves major corporations. American Express is one of Matrixx's customers.

As the significance of call centres is recognised, it is likely to have a growing impact on public services. Municipalities and government departments around the world are beginning to use call centres to manage incoming phone traffic, making use of CLI, comprehensive data warehouses and staff located in low wage cost regions. Central government may operate call centres at a distance from London. Local authorities in the south-east may also contract-out call handling so that they can take advantage of lower wage areas – this is already happening with some London boroughs.

But a major question is whether disparate public services have the vision to bring their activities together enough to allow single call centres to handle all public body enquiries in particular areas. The Society of Information Technology Management predicts that the future local authority will be equipped with a 24-hour call centre service, with staff using network computers to deal with any council business at any time of the day or night.

TELEWORKING

It is not only call centres that are taking work away from traditional geographic bases, and moving them to lower wage areas. Banks that used to employ data-inputting and data-processing staff in back offices in branches, now employ fewer staff who often work on industrial estates in dispersed regions.

This is called 'teleworking' – distance working based on telecommunications links. Although the public perception of teleworking is of home workers, plus office managers who are able to do much of their work from home, the reality is very different. Most teleworkers are actually rows of data-inputters sitting in what are effectively office factories, in highly organised and supervised environments.

Birmingham is one council that has allowed some of its staff to telework from home to reduce the need for office accommodation and car parking space. Newham has translators on call in their own homes, connected by video-conference facilities. This allows the council to pay

MANAGING GOVERNMENT

staff only when they are needed, and saves them spending most of their time travelling between council offices.

Teleworking has both benefits and drawbacks. It only suits staff who are highly motivated, though a survey conducted by British Telecom found that a typical UK organisation could save £2m by allowing 100 staff to work from home. BT, which stands to gain if more employers use teleworkers, argues that teleworking can increase motivation and efficiency among staff.

It also reduces the costs of operating central office accommodation. Where all staff do some work away from the office, employers can run a 'hot desk' system, where staff use any vacant desk, rather than have their 'own' spot in the office. There are clear environmental benefits, avoiding the pollution and congestion caused by commuting. The European Commission expects millions of people to become teleworkers over the next few years.

Some employers are integrating several of these modern working trends. Scottish Widows, for instance, has created the 'virtual call centre', a single phone number that connects to 70 staff working from home. The company says that its home teleworkers allow it to operate an out-of-office hours service using female former employees who left to have families. These are skilled, experienced and trusted individuals, who Scottish Widows wanted to bring back into its work force.

OUTSOURCING

Outsourcing is of far wider application than just for call centres. The computer functions of many government departments are now outsourced, with the US corporation EDS reportedly winning over half of government contracts, leading to some politicians voicing concerns at the strength of EDS in the public services market. This massive US corporation – established by former US presidential candidate Ross Perot, and bought and later disposed of by General Motors – has now won what is believed to be more than half of the Government's computing contracts.

EDS has been accused by some of its competitors of adopting predatory pricing, which could lead to future major price hikes at a time when only EDS will have the market position to win contract renewals. These allegations are strongly denied by EDS itself, which claims that it simply operates at lower costs than its competitors, while maintaining profitability on its public sector contracts.

The largest EDS contract is with the Inland Revenue, to run its computer services on a 10 year, £1.6bn contract. EDS has already slimmed back 13 data centres across the country to just three, and has transferred 2,100 civil servants into its own employment. EDS's internal staff newsletter stresses the prospects for integration and advancement for civil servants and local authority staff who transfer to the company along with their former employers' computer divisions.

EDS works on a price-per-transaction basis, converting what would have been capital costs into future revenue expenditure for the Government, and building into contracts strong incentives to achieve performance improvements. The corporation expects to halve transaction costs for tax returns by the end of the contract.

The point should be noted that the sheer capital investment required in modern ICT systems is creating a distorted market. Just as local authorities are no longer large enough to run computer departments that can, at least for the most part, compete against major private sector operators, so, too, the number of private sector suppliers of sufficient size to tender for major public contracts is diminishing. Even the very largest corporations must now enter into partnerships with other corporations to offer the expertise and financial security to compete for government business.

MANAGING GOVERNMENT

SECURITY

Computerisation should bring massive benefits to the public sector by reducing overhead costs. It also brings with it risks. One of these is service disruption in the event of computer breakdown – most obviously from the year 2000 problem, with many computers still not programmed to recognise the new millennium.

It is difficult to assess just how severe the year 2000 crisis will be – except to say that no one doubts that it is a crisis. Corporations have recruited experts to re-programme systems, to try to prevent widespread system shutdowns, and massive errors. If the year 2000 problem is not effectively handled, the costs associated with it could wipe out several years savings generated by computerisation.

A review by the Government's auditor, the National Audit Office, found that departments had reacted inadequately, and too slowly, in dealing with the year 2000 challenge.

The year 2000 problem stems from the fact that traditionally computers have been programmed not to recognise that the year is, say, 1997, but instead to read the year as '97'. When the year becomes 2000, the computer reads it as '00'. This might simply lead to a cancellation of some functions – in itself an enormous disruption of government and private sector business. But computers might also calculate that a benefit uprating to come into effect early in the year 2000 should be applied retrospectively over the previous century, giving rise to a massive overpayment. A few such overpayments and the DSS budget would be in a bad way.

The cost of putting this right is likely to be billions of pounds to industry, and the cost to government could approach this as well. In the United States a single state, Oregon, expects to spend over £50m putting the problem right.

Not only is there the potential for disruption, but the relevant programming skills are in short supply, pushing up wages for specialists to enormous heights. The particular demand is for programming expertise in the early computer languages, such as Cobol, which are not normally used today but which still form the basis of the software used on many mainframes on which many databases are stored. Oregon state has resorted to giving tax breaks to old programmers literally to come out of retirement to put right the problems created by their generation.

There are also major security threats that have not been properly addressed, according to reports from the Audit Commission and the Chartered Institute of Public Finance and Accountancy (Cipfa). A Cipfa report in 1996 found that one third of public bodies did not run regular checks to prevent virus entry into systems and databases. Even more worryingly, almost one half of public bodies have not reviewed network security.

This is of special concern, as it indicates that public organisations have ignored earlier warnings. A 1995 report from District Audit, which audits most councils and hospitals on behalf of the Audit Commission, said that network security controls were so lax that hackers working from home could enter some hospital computer systems, and might be able to interfere with intensive care controls. DA reported that one hospital worker had already gained unauthorised access to a computer system, and been able to alter the prescribed dose of a drug.

District Audit recommended very strongly that all public bodies should introduce stronger firewalls to prevent entry into their networks by hackers, and also establish proper security systems so that staff could only access those parts of systems they needed to access. Its study had found that in most hospitals and councils any person who had access to a hospital or council computer could obtain any information from any part of their computer system.

Confidential personal information obtained for a housing benefit claim could commonly be accessed, found DA, by any council worker in any department who just happened to be nosy. Similarly, sensitive information about domestic violence, and confidential information on child protection registers, could be inspected by staff who had no reason to access the computer files. Contractors doing work for public bodies had been able to use their clients' computers to obtain commercially sensitive information to help them prepare for future tenders.

Public bodies need to be more aware of the potential efficiency gains they can achieve from greater computerisation, and other applications of digital technology. It is equally true that they need to be more aware of the risks attached. Public managers still need to be better informed to make the most of the ICT revolution.

⑪ Government as regulator

PERIODS of enormous change inevitably present new and severe challenges. One of the most severe challenges to governments over the next few years is how to regulate the information and communication industry.

▲ ▲ ▲

There has been increasing discussion in Britain about whether the current separate regulatory regimes for telecommunications, television and the press remain appropriate, while these sectors are converging, and when it leaves the even more international medium of the Internet almost unregulated.

Convergence is a phenomenon that should not be underestimated. An illustration of the type of development we are going to see is an experiment that the *European* newspaper attempted. The *European* opened its own Web site with pages of text from the latest edition, combined with video footage to illustrate the story. The pages, like other Web sites, could be accessed via a telephone line and an Internet service provider, which might have been owned by a telecoms company, a computer software specialist, or a TV station, and the Internet edition could also be seen through Web TV.

If someone – who might be termed a reader, viewer or PC user – felt a report was in bad taste, who would they complain to? The

GOVERNMENT AS REGULATOR

Broadcasting Standards Commission, the Independent Television Commission, the Press Complaints Commission or Oftel, the Office of Telecommunications? It should be self-evident that where there is this amount of convergence between the industries, then the regulators equally need to converge. The failure by governments to recognise this can be taken as indictment on politicians generally in failing to understand in which direction the ICT industry is moving.

It might also be regarded as unfair and arbitrary that while British Telecom was prevented from offering TV services down phone lines, it was competing against cable companies offering both services, and that a sister company of Sky TV is a telecoms provider.

But if regulation in these areas is muddled, it is nothing to the problem of regulating the Internet. An example of the problem here is how governments have tackled, or more often not tackled, pornography on the Internet. Explicit pornography is available on Web sites and bulletin boards, some of which are accessed through Internet service providers, others by direct dialling.

Much of this pornography is far worse than the soft porn magazines available on the top shelves of some newsagents. To say that it is seriously deviant understates the more hard core material – there are images of sexual mutilation of women and children that any reasonable person would demand to be banned.

If we believe that at least some of this pornography, and also neo-nazi and racist material, should not be available on the Web, whose responsibility is it to control it? Many of the Internet service providers will not interfere unless there is strong pressure from governments to force them to do so.

But who is liable, and which government should enforce which laws? Should the legal responsibility rest only with the person or company who created the Web site? Should there be a further liability for the company that runs the host computer where the Web pages are situated? Should additional liability lie with the Internet service provider which allows users to access these pages? If an Internet service provider has a responsibility, which country's laws should be used against it, and in which country's courts should any action be heard? If a government fails to take action against operators in its country, should there be international sanctions against it, and of what kind?

Germany has taken the toughest line of the Western nations. Both the national government and state officials in Bavaria have carefully monitored material held on the Internet, and have been willing to take hard action. The Munich police force even has its own special unit for the investigation of the Internet to enforce the nation's normal regulations on the distribution of pornographic and neo-nazi material. Investigations are aided by the use of intelligent agents that seek out key words that hint at the dissemination of offensive material.

CompuServe is a United States corporation that offers direct on-line information services, and is also an Internet service provider. Crucially, CompuServe has a German division. It was the German division and its managing director that were charged with aiding the distribution of child pornography and neo-nazi publicity.

Had CompuServe not had a German division, action would have been much less straightforward. It is difficult to see how the German government could prevent its nationals from subscribing to an Internet service provider that is not based in Germany. Prohibition would not only be impractical, it would also be contrary to various international trade agreements.

A government might also use some form of surveillance system, if it could de-encrypt digital information flows, to detect what is being transmitted to people in its country. But this would not be a solution, as it is unlikely that it could be used instantly to close down transmission of banned material. Instead, it would be more useful in helping retrospectively to trace transmission and reception.

GOVERNMENT AS REGULATOR

Moreover, if governments insist that they can de-encrypt information for reasons of tackling offensive material, and to monitor serious organised crime, then this creates its own problems. The probability is that if encryption codes can be broken by governments then they can also be broken by hackers and criminals, undermining the move to use the Internet as a secure method of transacting business.

The most offensive Web sites have been created, and posted onto host computers, in countries that are outside the main trading blocks, some of which, such as Serbia, already suffer trade sanctions. Without bi-lateral support from those countries it is difficult to enforce regulations against offensive material being electronically communicated.

Some countries – notably China, but also some nations that are attempting electronic integration with the West such as Malaysia – are generally worried at the prospect of the Internet breaking down political as well as moral censorship. China has been successful, so far, in limiting its nationals' access to Western political bulletin boards and information sources, but this will be difficult to maintain as Chinese academic institutions and businesses make greater use of the Internet. But if China's restrictive system does work in the long term, many countries in the West will want to copy it to restrict access to pornography and racist material.

The Internet has created the environment within which far more international information exchange is possible. Non-governmental organisations in the UK find it very useful to obtain up-to-date information instantly from almost every country in the world, using a mixture of sources, including direct e-mail correspondence from agents in countries, bulletin boards containing the views of nationals, government statements put onto Web sites, and press and agency reports that can be read on Web sites.

Malaysia seems to have accepted that the liberalisation of information flows created by the Internet means that the country has to pay the price in greater political freedom, in return for attracting large inward investment programmes from major Western corporations.

The global character of the Internet also produces difficulties for electronic commerce. Which country's laws apply to a transaction over the Internet? The best legal advice is that it is the country where the buyer resides. This implies a requirement on the seller to know the address of the buyer, and to know the legal framework of that country. Companies that sell software that is down-loaded on-line, paid by credit card or by deductions from an electronic purse connected to a terminal, could complete a sale yet be unaware of the address of the purchaser, or the country whose laws govern that contract.

This is particularly important where the Internet is used for the sale of financial products. Banks that operate with licences in offshore financial centres may sell products to people in countries with very strong regulatory regimes. Resolving contractual disputes may prove very difficult. It underlines the need for a single international legal framework for commercial transactions, and for the need for a clear international trade agreement to clarify the role of national laws in relation to global electronic commerce. This is arguably a more important restriction on the operation of the Economic Union than the absence of a single currency, and one of the most pressing matters needing resolution in the field of international trade.

Internet service providers have a responsibility under an Organisation of Economic Co-operation Development agreement to ensure that all transactions conducted by their customers conform to the law. This, in practice, would be impossible to comply with – it is even more problematic given that the ISP market is about to be dominated by a few large corporations, with many small ISPs facing collapse and insolvency.

The locations of host computers used by companies and individuals for their e-mail addresses could also affect the legal basis of transactions they enter into. In many cases, this will mean that the laws of countries in which neither contractual party is based could affect the terms of a contract. Microsoft, for instance, is the ISP that many people in Europe use, yet it is based in the United States – and could be used by people, say, based in Britain and Morocco who are conducting trade with each other.

ELECTRONIC CRIME

Money laundering is another matter of pressing concern. Electronic money will assist money laundering in two ways. Firstly, holders of some kinds of electronic purse smart cards will be able to transfer money onto other purses, without any form of central monitoring, thereby preventing effective audit trails being established to monitor electronic cash handling. (This is not true of all types of electronic purses – some of which have centralised computer monitoring systems, to prevent purses being used for money laundering.) Secondly, the ease by which money can be transferred electronically from one account to another, almost from any country to any other at will, eases and speeds up the process of money transfer exponentially.

"It is very clear that money launderers will be using methods to place and layer funds in a manner that loses audit trails," says Dr James Backhouse, director of the Computer Security Research Centre at the London School of Economics.

Some of the big accountancy firms claim to have developed software that creates effective audit trails that will solve this problem, by allowing them instantly to trace the network of transactions that moves and launders stolen money. Dr Backhouse dismisses the suggestion that this will be effective. He believes that too many banks and other financial institutions will co-operate with criminals to hide illegally obtained money.

"Auditors have to make a living, and they are pumping a balloon when they talk in these terms," suggests Dr Backhouse. "Look at wire transfers today. Where banks, especially in North America, wire money from one bank to another they use a closed system, yet police investigators are unable to track over 90 per cent of dirty money sent through wire transfers."

Problems will worsen when electronic transfers are made by thousands of businesses and individuals, without necessarily using intermediaries. Many ISPs have begun offering transaction facilities in competition to banks. "There is no reason why issuers of electronic money need to be banks," points out Dr Backhouse. "Organised criminal groups are going to become ISPs, in the same way they run some banks in Russia and elsewhere. The whole system of regulation we have at the moment is going to be overtaken."

A colleague of Dr Backhouse at the LSE, Professor Ian Angell, has even gone so far as to argue that governments should ask whether they must give up trying to police commercial transactions, and recognise that people and gangs will go about doing business in their own way and avoid state interference. "The nation state is dead. The end of progressive taxation is in sight," Professor Angell told a conference on cyberspace money laundering.

Professor Angell went on to suggest the concept of what he terms 'off-planet commerce', whereby many transactions will occur 'in the ether', outside the control and territory of any nation. A further complication could arise if Professor Angell's science fiction speculation becomes accurate. He suggests that future satellites, containing host computers, might be launched by multinational corporations that refuse to accept the authority of any government. Which state, he asks, could then regulate or tax the state-less cyber-corporation of the future?

Quoting the famous tax avoider Leona Helmsley, Professor Angell believes that in the future "only the little people will pay taxes". He concludes that "Democracy will mutate into an irrelevancy. The 'will of the people' voting for full employment, a minimum wage and fair

GOVERNMENT AS REGULATOR

taxation is merely turkeys voting for Christmas."

"Territory is now meaningless," agrees Dr Backhouse. "I don't see how regulation can work. The whole underpinning of regulation is going to rot away, and rapidly. Electronic commerce is the driver, and electronic money is the means. Once you have got a critical mass of electronic commerce using legitimate money it will be very easy for dirty money, used electronically, to nestle among the leaves.

"It is early days, but we have seen how quickly the Internet has taken off, and it is only a matter of time before the teething problems of electronic money are overcome, and the way will be open for moving value away from one country to another."

THE END OF TAXATION?

Moving value will be aided by the evolution of offshore financial centres, operating as commercial 'flags of convenience'. Added to devices such as promissory notes and barter, it is likely that people and corporations committed to tax evasion will have the ready means of achieving it at their finger tips.

The idea that states will soon be without income is one that governments must take seriously, according to Rowan Bosworth-Davies, a former fraud squad officer who is now a senior consultant specialising in electronic crime and tax avoidance with international law firm Titmuss Sainer Dechert. He believes that most politicians, lawyers and bankers are unforgivably ignorant of the disaster that may befall them within a few years.

The problem of money laundering is much less important than the one of how governments will continue to function without income, suggests Mr Bosworth-Davies. "The big issue is how democracies will fund themselves. How will they raise the money for welfare needs?

GOVERNMENT IN THE DIGITAL AGE

People now have the ability to emigrate electronically, and re-create themselves in an economic sort of cyberspace. This is where problems will lie because societies will no longer be able to finance the concept of government."

Taken to its logical conclusion, electronic money could destroy the concept of society as we know it, believes Mr Bosworth-Davies. "When governments can't tax you anyway, it knocks out their reasons for existence," he suggests.

It is realistic to imagine a multinational corporation that has offices in several countries including Britain, having a main e-mail address in Malaysia, transacting electronically with countries in every continent. Goods may be held in several parts of the world.

Which country's tax regime will apply? How can governments prevent transactions being nominally conducted from the country with the lowest corporation tax?

One of the initiatives the Malaysian government intends to implement is to create an ICT development and enterprise zone in one region, where the country would forego tax in return for investment from corporations basing themselves there. Many of the world's leading ICT corporations – including Microsoft, Netscape, Compaq and IBM – are involved in the scheme, and are advising the government there. If they actually or nominally move their operations to Malaysia, the West's tax income could fall dramatically, and could lead to a big 'corporation drain'.

Transfer pricing – artificially distorted pricing mechanisms for transactions between the divisions in different countries of multinational corporations, to enable them to declare profits in countries with the lowest tax regimes – will become more common, and will be used by small companies as well as the largest. Similarly, electronic commerce will open up international sourcing of products and services to small firms, accelerating trade globalisation.

GOVERNMENT AS REGULATOR

Individuals, too, may work transnationally. The flexible labour market has been recognised as a reality by today's governments. An element of this is workers operating a portfolio of jobs. This has been criticised by trade unions as undermining job security. It also creates an opportunity for higher paid workers to avoid tax altogether.

Workers of the future will work even more at the computer terminal, and this may affect middle class professions such as accountants and architects as much as data processors. They are likely to be based in different countries from their employers. Whether the contractual arrangements are for the person to be employed on a staff or a self-employed basis, the prospects for tax avoidance are greatly increased.

Individuals may find themselves working for different employers on each day of the week, with each employer based, for tax purposes at least, in a different country. In each of those countries the employee may be below the taxable income threshold, and be able to avoid tax in each. Taxation authorities may find it impossible to check on the real earnings of self-employed people, with clients based in a range of countries.

There will be other problems for the tax authorities. Tax evasion is most commonly detected, not from employers' records that indicate that salaries have been paid out untaxed, but from observation of the spending patterns of high illicit earners. What has been spent must, presumably, have been earned.

The ability of the Inland Revenue to detect untaxed income will accordingly be undermined when most products can be purchased internationally on-line, away from the prying eyes of tax inspectors.

Another problem for governments is how to control transactions that eschew hard currency. Local exchange and trading schemes have been established in Australia, Canada and Britain, and similar schemes exist in the United States, with varying degrees of success. One of the factors holding them back has been that they typically operate from out-of-date hard copy directories. If they used electronic information, accessed either from home terminals or from public access kiosks, they might take off in a bigger way, and help the exchange of redundant equipment as well as assist out-of-work people to trade services.

But a system of barter exchange would be difficult to police. While it leads theoretically to a tax liability, participants may choose not to declare barter income and in all likelihood they would get away with it. Furthermore, how could a tax authority determine the real value of a simple exchange of redundant equipment that had no book value to the people or corporations concerned? Barter trade between corporations is now an important factor in United States commerce, mostly featuring stocks and services that have little book value.

THE BIT TAX

One option, considered by both the European Commission and the United States government, is to tax all transference of electronic information, the so-called 'bit tax' proposal. The principle behind it is to overcome both lost tax revenues, as electronic systems allow businesses and people to hide levels of taxable trade, and also the loss of jurisdiction, termed by some 'the dilution of territory'.

The expectation is that within an electronic world, neither taxes on income (whether they be income tax or corporation tax) nor taxes on transactions (such as value added tax) can be reliably collected. It will be impossible to prove what income a person or corporation genuinely has achieved, or what service transactions take place. As transactions become global, the taxation bureaux and the accountancy profession will find it increasingly difficult to undertake effective audits.

If we cannot verify what activities are taking place, the argument goes, it is better to find an alternative system of taxation that is

GOVERNMENT AS REGULATOR

verifiable. The obvious solution is to tax per parcel of information despatched, using the Internet service providers as an obligatory agent of the state to assist with tax collection.

Proposals also attempt to deal with the problem, outlined by the OECD, that official productivity statistics fail to recognise the efficiency benefits realised by information technology. It is also argued by European Commission advisors Luc Soete and Karin Kamp, of Maastricht University, that ICT is the cause of a serious distortion in economic performance indicators. They suggest that inflation figures treat investment in technology purely as cost, without also reflecting its greater performance capability and the savings which result – leading to inappropriate and unnecessary attempts by central banks and governments to deflate economies.

Soete and Kamp report that in 1995 alone, the US government lost over $3bn in tax revenues from sales conducted via the Internet, which are treated as mail orders and are therefore tax exempt. They went on to argue that while European governments do not have the same tax loopholes, they do have others. VAT is avoided, they suggest, through global electronic access to financial and telephone services, which can be based in low-tax or zero-tax countries. Further, with services provided on-line, there will be a reduction in the size of the distribution industry, leading to further loss of tax revenues.

"The main economic argument for a shift in the tax base away from tangibles towards intangibles is thus simple," wrote Soete and Kamp. "Just as one to two hundred years ago, economic discussions were dominated by the 'corn tax', reflecting the importance of grain for the national economy, today, the dominant issue should be how governments can adjust their tax base in line with the changing economic structure towards an information society and the increasing importance of information transmission for economic production and consumption. Shifting tax revenues on the basis of a tax on the individual electronic 'bits' or 'bytes' appears from the outset the most straightforward and logical taxing method."

Rates of tax proposed by Soete and Kamp and others would be in the region of one cent per megabit, which would generate taxes that might be equivalent to about four per cent of gross domestic product of a European nation. The cost to the consumer would be less than a penny for a half hour session downloading from World Wide Web sites, or about 0.1 per cent of profits for a major ICT corporation.

These figures, though, look optimistic, and will need to be closely examined by economists if governments are serious about implementing the proposals.

But a bit tax is likely to be open to avoidance, through the use of host computer systems based in zero tax or low tax economies operating as new offshore financial centres. Its applicability is in any case limited to where it can be measured – it might mean that cable-connected messages would be taxed, while those based on radio-telephony and satellite transmission would be exempt, which would be an absurd distortion.

It is difficult to be confident that all the Internet service providers will co-operate. Some commentators are predicting that large criminal gangs will soon establish their own Internet services providers, recognising that their potential role for money laundering is at least as great as that of banks.

Enforcement of a cybertax could be as problematic as the taxes it replaces. And it would build additional overheads into activities that governments need to promote in order to achieve international competitiveness. If it became more expensive to transact electronically than by traditional means, it might simply push some countries' businesses into using old-fashioned business systems for a longer period, ensuring that their companies' systems are obsolescent, reducing that country's international competitiveness, and increasing the rate of business failure.

GOVERNMENT AS REGULATOR

Another superficially attractive possibility is to integrate electronic transactions into a taxation system, so that all business deals in cyberspace have to be processed via a government department. If they were circumscribed within an agreed electronic framework, where payments were instantly transferred and a percentage was allocated to the taxation authority at the electronic point of sale, then the collection of tax would become much simpler and cheaper, and governments would be paid sooner.

The difficulty with this, of course, is that it creates a new form of government bureaucracy, where it monitors each transaction and again relies on the honesty of the parties involved. Electronic communication and electronic commerce do not need an Internet service provider as an intermediary. One business can direct dial another business, order goods or services, and arrange to supply other goods or services in return, and the deal is pretty well done and dusted without any state involvement. Similarly, Internet service providers cannot be relied upon to co-operate.

A solution might be for governments to vet all electronic communications, but this again faces the problem of encryption, and, in any case, is unlikely to be politically acceptable in most Western countries. And the sheer burden of information transfer, even allowing for the use of artificial intelligence to analyse transactions, might make such activities an ineffective means of policing revenue collection.

The difficulties attached to any form of cybertaxation have been recognised by President Clinton. He appears to have recognised that, at least for the time being, a bit tax would be unenforceable, and would create perverse incentives for United States industry – either driving it away from new technology, or encouraging US corporations to re-locate to more fiscally liberal countries.

President Clinton has announced that he will take a 'hands-off' approach to Internet regulation. This led David Barratt, marketing director for Internet service provider UUNet to prophesy that the

Internet will become "the largest free trade zone in the world".

Some political analysts argue that governments will simply have to accept that most of their taxation income will dry up in coming years, and learn to spend less. Others say that because this is politically unacceptable, a solution will have to be found – but admit they have not come up with one yet.

Experts are increasingly arguing that these factors mean that taxation will have to move away from the mobile aspects of production – capital and enterprise – and focus on the inanimate, or near inanimate – namely labour and land. This means that ideas of fair or progressive taxation would have to be abandoned, and regressive taxation imposed instead. It may even mean that poorer workers, who are the least mobile, will end up paying the highest rates of tax. These are ideas that would be anathema to socialist and social democrat politicians everywhere, but alternatives are hard to find.

DILEMMAS FOR POLITICIANS AND BANKERS

"A revolution in communications technology has facilitated a worldwide counter-revolution in public policy," wrote Gerald Epstein in 'International Capital Mobility and the Scope for National Economic Management'. "At the push of a button, financial capital moves around the globe at such an amazing speed that national governments seem helpless in its wake.

"Legislatures and citizens who want to buck the trend and achieve goals of high employment, egalitarian development and sustainable growth are paralysed by the threat that any policy which lowers the rate of profit will cause capital to be moved to more profitable environs, thereby reducing investment and lowering the community's standard of living" (from *States against Markets*, edited by Boyer and Drache).

GOVERNMENT AS REGULATOR

These issues should worry the Bank of England and other central banks, faced with responsibility for monetary and inflation control, at least as much as politicians concerned about fiscal policy. As Internet banks and the Internet service providers undertake transactions electronically, away from central banking monitoring, so there is a risk that they effectively increase the amount of money in circulation – especially in the case of global currencies such as the Dollar and the Euro.

This has led the Banking, Insurance and Finance Union to conclude that electronic commerce will create what it calls 'a second electronic banking industry', which will issue currency on an unregulated basis. This issuing of 'virtual money' could create an inflationary and monetary crisis for 'real money'.

BIFU has consequently called for the establishment of an 'electronic mint', which would oversee electronic exchange controls, determine whether there should be limits for transfers between electronic purses, and whether people should be prevented from transferring money held on a purse in one country onto purses and accounts in other countries.

If the complex issues of territoriality can be overcome, there are a stack of other regulatory issues that governments need to address. At the top of these is the need to ensure equality of access to the telecommunications infrastructure.

This is not a simple rich versus poor question. In practice, it may not be impoverished inner city families that are without access to the Internet, once digital TV is affordable and Web TV is accessible via cable. It may be more of an issue in rural areas, where cable companies and BT may be reluctant to run ISDN standard cables unless they are paid to do so. The economic future of rural areas is partially dependent on the quality of communications which can be achieved by satellite and radio-wave systems.

There is, of course, no practical reason why telecoms companies should not operate differential pricing policies across the country. After all, this has been adopted by other utility operators. The water industry, in the hands of regional private companies, charges according to the actual costs of water distribution. Electricity and gas are also likely to become increasingly expensive in the 'Celtic fringes' compared to the home counties, reflecting both the economies of scale achieved in high demand urban centres, and the costs of operating a broad distribution network.

What social effects this will have we will have to wait to see. It may help to reinforce the existing trend towards rural areas being taken over by rich and retired families, who are not economically active but who can afford a more expensive lifestyle.

On the other hand, if the financial costs of living in the regional extremities gets too great, we may actually see a reversal of the process. The middle classes may be driven out of rural areas, pushing down home prices, and creating new pockets of deprivation and poverty, with little access to jobs and wealth-creating activities. Either scenario is unlikely to promote the rural countryside as a vibrant place for young adults to live and work.

Governments will therefore have to consider whether one of the conditions for licensing of telecoms and interactive TV operators will be the need to provide a standard service at a single price across the whole of the UK.

We are likely to see the establishment of a number of alliances between broadcasters and telecoms operators, which will throw up further dilemmas for policy makers. Will it be acceptable for joint enterprises to be dominant within particular countries? How will governments regulate these joint enterprises which operate across boundaries? When some services are provided via satellite technology, what is the regulatory role of individual governments?

There is a further problem for governments that continue to have

GOVERNMENT AS REGULATOR

state-owned broadcasters. In future broadcasting will be increasingly global, with any TV station being able to be received anywhere in the world.

Could the British government justify the continued public-funding of the BBC if the majority of its audience was outside the UK? Perhaps state funding should be ring-fenced for particular activities, encouraging the BBC to operate more revenue-generating operations aimed at overseas audiences. But if governments, rather than an operator, fund activities, should they put out to tender the public service element for all broadcasters to bid? In which case, the BBC could presumably be privatised to generate funds for the Government. And what will be the relationship with the BBC once it enters into a joint venture with a privately owned, possibly foreign based, telecoms company?

There may not be any simple answers to all these problems, but at the very least governments must recognise the size of the challenge they are facing. Judging by the comments made by politicians so far, few understand the task facing them.

⑫ The future of government

GOVERNMENT is today facing three key questions. 'What is the job of government?', 'How can it best do that job?', and 'How can it pay for it?' In answering those questions governments must start with a clean sheet of paper.

▲ ▲ ▲

There are two driving forces that require politicians to re-think their approach. The first is competition in industrial markets from the Pacific Rim countries, the so-called tiger economies, several of which have been increasing their gross domestic product by nearly 10 per cent *per annum* over recent years. Tax rates, wages and public spending are all much lower in the East than in the West.

The second factor, which is closely attached to the first, is that new technology delivers services in a different way from old technology. It is less labour-intensive, faster and cheaper. If the West is to compete with the East, it must invest heavily to convert its public services to take better advantage of digital technology.

It is not simply a matter of entering into joint ventures with the private sector and purchasing new computer systems. To obtain the most from a new generation of equipment, the whole apparatus of government is likely to need to be re-engineered in at least as radical a

THE FUTURE OF GOVERNMENT

way as business has been.

The British government will need to slim down its hierarchies further. It will also need to improve its information flows within and between departments, and with the outside world. But it must do far more.

Government must decide whether the existing boundaries between government departments and with agencies continue to be appropriate. The Computing Services and Software Association believes that government departments should be shuffled so that public services are delivered in a seamless way, with departments organised to focus on services and the means of delivery, rather than accepting traditional divisions.

One example is the diffused way in which our personal financial relationship with government is conducted. We must provide similar information to a variety of public bodies to determine our tax liabilities and benefit entitlement. A person who moves in and out of work might be in regular communication with the Inland Revenue, the Contributions Agency, the Benefits Agency, the Department of Education and Employment, plus the local authority's council tax collection department, its council tax benefit section and its housing benefit section. The person might apply on separate forms, for tax rebates, unemployment benefit, sickness benefit, income support, single person benefit, housing benefit and council tax benefit, and perhaps, even, education grants.

The question has to be asked whether this is a sensible way to conduct relations between the citizen and the state. It certainly does not assist the Government to achieve its objective of creating a flexible labour market, enabling people to move easily between welfare and work and back again if necessary. Electronic service delivery offers a marvellous opportunity to rationalise the numbers of layers of contact, saving the cost of bureaucracy while also improving the take-up of state benefits. Coincidentally, it should also reduce the amount of fraud and accidental errors in the payment of benefits.

Other criticisms of government made by the ICT industry are that the British physical infrastructure has become out of date, and with it the skills base of much of the state sector. This is particularly evident, it says, in the class room, where teachers are often not fully ICT-literate, and where there are inadequate numbers of PCs for pupils to learn how to use them properly.

The view of the CSSA is that the previous British government did too little for the ICT industry. In particular, they complained, it failed to ensure that the labour force was ICT-skilled, it failed to offer adequate tax breaks to ICT-investors and it failed to persuade UK venture capitalists to invest in the ICT industry.

While it is clear that education remains a government responsibility, many would deny that the state should be held accountable for industrial decisions. The CSSA view is that the more pro-active approach taken by the Irish government, in terms of tax breaks and in creating a highly skilled workforce, led to it becoming the most attractive investment destination in Europe for US ICT corporations.

An even more explicit example of government intervention to promote ICT investment is in Malaysia. The country's prime minister, Mahithir Mohamad, has lobbied multinational corporations extensively to invest in a multimedia super-corridor, based on a planned new 300 square mile, $40bn, super-city to be called Cyberjaya – which will eventually replace Kuala Lumpur as the country's capital.

The new city will contain a multimedia university, a fully electronic paperless central government, and each home will have the most modern broadband connections for telecommunications and interactive TV. Smart identity cards will be the basis of communication between state and citizen, just as telemedicine will be the standard means of contact between GP and patient.

To assist with the project, Malaysia is being advised by the top

THE FUTURE OF GOVERNMENT

management consultants McKinsey, and has created a 30-member advisory panel, with membership including Bill Gates of Microsoft and others from Oracle, Netscape, Apple, IBM, Sony, Nippon, Compaq, Sun, Siemens and Motorola. In return for membership, the corporations are entitled to a 10 year tax holiday, a waiver on restrictions on the employment of foreign nationals, and, contrary to normal rules, divisions based in Malaysia can be wholly owned by foreigners. It has also lifted normal censorship rules for foreign corporations.

Malaysia is launching a second stock exchange, devoted to small ICT companies, whether locally or foreign owned, to assist in raising equity stakes. The existing Kuala Lumpur stock exchange is buoyant, and the alternative exchange is expected to be a success.

Despite all this, in some aspects Malaysia still lags behind its neighbour Singapore, which has connected all its homes to interactive TV and the Internet; has already converted its identity cards into smart cards; and has a network of multimedia kiosks across the island city, supplied by the private sector, but which connect citizen to government.

If our competitors in the future really are the Pacific tiger economies we can conclude that we are currently behind Singapore and Malaysia in the race. No wonder that a European Commission report says that Europe's governments and businesses are not yet ready for ICT.

The information revolution will, once we have the benefit of historical perspective, be recognised as equally significant to the industrial revolution. But the changes brought about by the industrial revolution were not just technical, they were also social and economic.

Rich landowners found themselves poorer than upstart entrepreneurs who saw the future clearly. Men who ruled their homes with a rod of iron, making their wives and children work like slaves for them, were suddenly forced out of the micro factory within the home, into the mass factory in the mill, where they were locked in to prevent them going to the pub and getting drunk. Many poor families got poorer, just as some

GOVERNMENT IN THE DIGITAL AGE

poor countries became poorer.

Any revolution has its winners and losers. Britain won in the industrial revolution, but it may become a loser in the information revolution. Our future place in the world will be determined partially by decisions taken by the global multinationals, partly by the quality of leadership of our own government.

In the same way that our national government must plan for our place in the world, so, too, municipal governments must plot a direction for our cities and our countryside. We can expect to see new areas of deprivation, but we cannot yet say whether the countryside will lose out from poor transport and communication links.

If rural areas have full access to the information superhighway, we may instead find that cities become ever poorer and more depopulated. The supermarket chains have, to a large extent, moved themselves away from the old city centres, driving out much of the commercial heart of the cities. Now the same chains are competing in other sectors, offering banking, shopping, holidays, electricity and gas at a cheaper price to their best customers. They have begun offering home shopping through the Internet, and we can expect that they will soon meet our full range of needs through Web sites. In the future we will be able to live, work and shop without leaving our own homes.

The highly competitive interest rates on current accounts offered by the supermarkets will probably force many banks out of the market, and bank and building society branches will in any case close when customers opt to save money by doing their banking at home.

Councillors in local authorities should have a look at their high streets and think what they will look like in a virtual world. The banks and building societies will be replaced by the virtual bank; grocery stores by home shopping or out-of-town supermarkets; book shops by Web sites; and music shops by other Web sites. What will be left of the city centre? Perhaps nothing but cheap homes, theme pubs and empty car parks.

THE FUTURE OF GOVERNMENT

There is then the threat of new methods of conflict between nations, or by terrorists. The nature of warfare will change dramatically over forthcoming decades. Weapons systems will be integrated into computer systems, with the risk of dehumanising the process of war. Will a generation of people brought up on computer games that give them the option of deleting the enemy, take the reality of screen-based warfare sufficiently seriously?

Claims for the accuracy of Cruise missiles during the Gulf War may have been over-stated, but are a fair reflection of the way war might be fought. Missiles can be guided by satellites to improve accuracy, making pre-emptive strikes more likely and putting the world permanently on the edge of major conflict. As Iran moves towards nuclear capability, will the United States hold back from wiping out its near-completed missiles?

The latest interface between fighter/bomber planes or Cruise missiles with satellites, promises to make bombing an ever more accurate process. Global Positioning System (GPS) satellites can guide missiles with pinpoint accuracy to a target, and using digitised on-board cameras the missiles can seek an identical match on the ground to the satellites' identified target. This, it is believed, should allow missiles to hit an exact window of a building using a missile launched from over 100 miles away.

Hot and cold wars may soon be conducted through computer systems, played as if they were computer games, but producing massive economic impact on the real world. Nations are training computer experts in how to disrupt the information and communication infrastructures of other countries, in ways that may hide the culprits. The United States' National Security Agency employs hundreds of staff to protect the country from information warfare. A US government report on information warfare found that the country risked a 'national security disaster' because it has become over-dependent on computer systems, and to reduce that risk would cost at least $3bn.

Hackers might disable air traffic control systems and implant computer viruses into anything, from government departments' administrative systems, to stock exchange trading systems, to electricity generators' demand monitoring systems. Electro-magnetic pulses and microwave beams could disrupt broadcasting and other communication networks. Recognition of these factors led to the structure of the Internet, as a decentralised link that cannot be destroyed by one hit on a single computer.

If there are still 'traditional' wars in the future, even these will be different. Battle field commanders will benefit from the information revolution. Instead of relying on liaison officers, dodging flak, to bring back news some hours later of what is taking place on the ground, commanders will see the war as it is happening through video cameras using satellite communication, allied to the visual reports from satellite spy systems.

Opponents of the future may not simply be other nations, but modern guerrilla armies, armed not with armalites, but with a very good hacker instead. The cause might not be independence for a beleaguered community, but animal rights or freedom from tax authorities. The rise of the American militias gives us an idea how the future could also unfold in the UK.

Neil Barrett, a consultant with Bull Information Systems, wrote in a paper called 'Information Warfare' of the risks to the structure of society from hackers, gangs and outlaw states. "The Internet was developed to ensure that US military communications could not be entirely destroyed in the event of conflict; the concern now is that it can support a more insidious, invisible and damaging threat to the very infrastructure it was developed to protect."

A sophisticated hacker – who might also be a terrorist or represent an enemy nation – might replicate the hardware fault that in 1991 caused an AT&T phone system to collapse, which led to 500 air flights being cancelled, stranding 85,000 passengers, and causing losses of hundreds

THE FUTURE OF GOVERNMENT

of thousands of dollars, suggested Mr Barrett.

"During the build-up to the Gulf War," wrote Neil Barrett, "an experiment was performed at Bollings Air Force base, Massachusetts. A convicted hacker was persuaded to test the security surrounding key US Air Force systems. During the most sensitive and critical stage of the Coalition's operations this hacker managed to break into, not a handful, or even a dozen systems, but over 200. Not one of the sites noticed it had been attacked; the damage could have been crippling."

In another incident, an Air Force captain was able, using a basic PC and an ordinary Internet account, to gain control of a US Navy computer on a warship that was the flagship for a sailing fleet. "If this facility can be exploited by enemies, in time of war, then this could shift the balance of power – from a count of warheads, men and munitions – to keyboards, modems and software," argued Mr Barrett. More optimistically, in times of international terrorism, governments might make positive use of electronic communication by directly contacting all its citizens in a particular country, either by e-mail or through interactive TV, to warn them confidentially of forthcoming danger, advising them of evacuation plans.

Planning for the future is simple during a period of stability. It is during periods of rapid change that management and policy development is difficult. The revolution that is taking place around us offers the most difficult political challenge of our lifetimes.

We do not know where we are going, and the speed of technological development is so great that we cannot even say with certainty where we want to go. Politicians coping with new technology at the turn of the new century might feel like rodeo riders: the best they can hope for is probably just to stay on board. But the dream remains that they might actually tame the beast.

BIBLIOGRAPHY

Andrew Adonis, speech to Demos conference, 'Life After Politics', London, 1997.

Ian Angell, 'The shape of things to come', speech to 'Cyberlaundering and fraud' conference, Lisbon, 1997.

Daniele Archibugi and Jonathan Michie (eds.), *Technology, Globalisation and Economic Performance*, Cambridge: Cambridge University Press, 1997.

Neil Barrett, *The State of the Cybernation*, London: Kogan Page, 1996.

Neil Barrett, *Digital Crime*, London: Kogan Page, 1997.

Neil Barrett, 'Information warfare', private paper, 1997.

Theodore L. Becker, 'Electrifying Democracy', London: *Demos quarterly*, issue 3, 1994.

Christopher Bellamy, 'Britain's defences down against cyber-warriors', *The Independent*, 13th March, 1997.

Peter Blair and Steven Hedges, 'NetWorking', London: Association of District Councils, 1997.

Robert Boyer and Daniel Drache, *States Against Markets*, London: Routledge, 1996.

British Medical Journal, editorial, 23rd July, 1994, quoted in *Demos quarterly*, 4/1994.

Alan Burkitt-Gray, 'The intelligent island: Singapore's go-ahead, high technology community', *Electronic Government International* magazine, October, 1996.

Alan Burkitt-Gray, 'The laptop democracy: all eyes focused on Brazil', *Electronic Government International* magazine, October, 1996.

Dave Carter, 'Creative Cities and the Information Society', Manchester: Manchester City Council, 1997.

Chancellor to the Duchy of Lancaster, 'Government.Direct', London: Stationery Office, 1996.

Chartered Institute of Public Finance and Accountancy, 'IT audit in public service organisations', London: CIPFA, 1996.

GOVERNMENT IN THE DIGITAL AGE

Choy-Peng Shah, 'Something for everyone: Singapore's electronic government programme', *Electronic Government International* magazine, November, 1996.

Computing Software and Services Association, 'The IT Manifesto', London: CSSA, 1997.

Economist, 'Virtually fantastic: Malaysia's information ambitions', 1st March, 1997.

Economist, 'The future of warfare', 8th March, 1997.

Economist, 'Disappearing taxes', 31st May, 1997.

European Commission, 'Europe and the global information society: recommendations to the European Council', 1994.

European Commission, 'European Digital Cities', proceedings of the 1st conference, Copenhagen, May 1996.

European Commission, 'Networks for People and their Communities', first annual report from the Information Society Forum, 1996.

Bill Gates, *The Road Ahead*, London: Penguin, 1995.

Paul Gosling, *Financial Services in the Digital Age*, London: Bowerdean, 1996.

Eric Hobsbawm, *The Age of Revolution*, London: Cardinal, 1988.

ICL, 'The informed society', Slough: ICL, 1997.

ICL and the Civil Service College, 'The effects of the information revolution on governance', London: ICL, 1997.

Justice, 'Response by Justice to the green paper 'Government.Direct'', London: Justice, 1997.

James Kynge, 'Mahithir woos America's IT giants', *Financial Times*, 26th February, 1997.

Howard M. Leichter, 'Democratic cures: the lessons from Oregon', London: *Demos quarterly*, issue 3, 1994.

Francis A McDonough, 'A glimpse into the 21st century', *Electronic Government International* magazine, February, 1997.

Lisa Macfarlane and Peter Lees, 'Barred facts', *Health Service Journal*, 13th March, 1997.

Geoff Mulgan (ed.), *Life After Politics*, London: Demos, 1997.

BIBLIOGRAPHY

Janie Percy-Smith, 'Digital Democracy', London: Commission for Local Democracy, 1995.

Marcus Pollett, 'Home comforts in Orlando', *Electronic Government International* magazine, January 1997.

Reed Personnel Services, '1,000 ideas for the next government', London: Reed, 1997.

Daniel Sabbagh, 'Self-health and the virtual health service', London: *Demos quarterly*, issue 4, 1994.

Steven S Smith and Glenda Morgan, 'Parliaments on-line', *Electronic Government International* magazine, October, 1996.

Luc Soete and Karin Kamp, 'The bit tax: the case for further research', Maastricht: University of Maastricht, 1996.

Statewatch, European Union and the FBI launch global surveillance system, London: Statewatch, 1997.

Frederick Studemann, 'Bavaria gives lead in cleaning Net', *Financial Times*, 30th April, 1997.

Karen Swinden (ed.), 'Tomorrow's Town Hall', London: Kable/Local Government Management Board, 1995.

Simon Wallace, 'The future's bright: the future's digital', London: The King's Fund, 1996.

Simon Wallace and Ricky Richardson, 'Telemedicine in the UK for the Millennium and Beyond', Cardiff: WorldCare UK, 1997.

Brian Westcott (ed.), 'IT trends in local government 1996/97', Northampton: Society of Information Technology Management.

Ian Williams, 'Spain gets smart social security', *Electronic Government International* magazine, February, 1997.

David Windle, 'Missile puts pilots clear of danger', *Sunday Times*, 12th January, 1997.

INDEX

Adam Smith Institute 71
Adonis, Andrew 24
Advanced Trans-European Telematics Applications for Community Help (Attach) 28
Alaska Legislative Teleconference 29
alienation 84-6
Angell, Ian 132
artificial intelligence (AI) 37, 41, 72, 73
ATM (asynchronous transfer mode) 8, 56, 81, 96, 104
Australia 135
Australian Cultural Network 94
Australian Museums On-Line Service 94
Automated Traffic Offence Management System 33

Backhouse, Dr James 131, 132, 133
Bank of England 140
banking, on-line 99
Banking, Insurance and Finance Union 141
barcodes, used by hospitals 62
Barratt, David 139
Barrett, Neil 150, 151
barter exchange 136
BBC 142
benefit transfer, electronic 68
benefits fraud 72
bit tax 136-40
black box recorders 36-7
bloodhounds (intelligent agents) 46, 116
Bollings Air Force base, Massachusetts 151
Bologna 30
Bosworth-Davies, Rowan 133, 134
Brazil 19-20
Britain 135
tomorrow 35-9
British Airways 118
British Medical Association 60-1
British Telecom 102, 121, 127
broadcasting 142, 143
bus stops, electronic displays at 46

call centres 116-20
caller line identification (CLI) 118-19
Cambridge 18, 75
Canada 135
car share schemes 50
CCTV cameras 19, 36, 37, 38
CD-ROM 57, 58, 89, 90
Central Information Technology Unit (CITU) 8, 96, 103, 111, 112, 113, 114

Chartered Institute of Public Finance and Accountancy (Cipfa) 124
Chauffeur 50
Chelmsley Wood library 26-7
China 129
CITU *see* Central Information Technology Unit (CITU)
Clarke, Kenneth 13-14, 99
CLI (caller line identification) 118-19
Clinton, President 139
commerce 104, 115-16
and the digital infrastructure 106
electronic 115-16, 130
and World Wide Web 116
Commonwealth, English language ties 118
Community Users Information (Cousin) 93
Compaq 134
Compuserve 47, 128
Computing Services and Software Association (CSSA) 85, 101, 111, 112, 115, 145, 146
congestion, management of 47-51
congestion mapping systems 47
convergence 126, 127
Crawford, Philip 85, 103
crime, electronic 131-3
Croydon library 89
Cyberjaya 146
cybertaxation 138, 139

data matching 70, 71, 99-100
Data Protection Registrar 39, 70, 71
data warehouse 67, 119
data-wells 62
databases, phone directory and address 119
de-encrypting, of information 129
Denison, David 104, 114
Department of Communications and the Arts (Australia) 94
Department of Education and Employment 111, 145
Department of Environment, Transport and the Regions 48, 110, 111
Department of National Heritage 111
Department of Trade and Industry 112
diabetes sufferers, distance monitoring for 55
digital cameras, on motorways 36
digital cities 96
digital computer identification system 35-6
digital infrastructure 100, 101, 106
digital technology 8
distance learning 83
District Audit 124
DocGuide 60-1

INDEX

Drivers and Vehicle Licensing Agency 36, 68, 99
DSS 14, 67, 71, 100, 111

e-mail discussion groups 82
EDS 38, 121, 122
educational system, learning based 81
Eftpos (electronic funds transfer at point-of-sale) 102
electronic benefit transfer 68
electronic commerce 115-16, 130, 139
electronic communication 139
electronic crime 131-3
electronic democracy 16-30
electronic house calls 54
electronic infrastructure 104
electronic mint 141
electronic payment system 91
electronic prescribing 61
electronic purse smart cards 131-3
electronic purses 8
electronic signalling systems 47
electronic ticket selling 67
electronic tolling 49
Electronic Town Meetings 29
electronic transfers 131-2
electronic travel information systems 46
Electronic Village Halls 28-9
electronic voting 11, 12, 17, 19, 20, 24
Elmore, John 112
encryption 41, 129, 139
Epstein, Gerald 140
Estonia 105
European, The 126
European Commission 14, 25, 27, 29, 50, 61, 69, 83, 84, 89-90, 95, 104, 105-6, 136, 147
European Digital Cities 29
Experian 71

facial mapping 35
fingerprint readers 50, 91
firewalls 41
First Direct 117
France 62
fraud detection 73-4, 100, 110, 145
FSN's Democracy Network 18-19
Full Service Network (FSN) 18
future 33-5
(2008) 10-12, 31-2, 43-4, 52-3, 64-5, 77-8, 87
governments in the 144-51
health in the 52-63
legal systems in the 31-2
transport in the 43-51

future *see also* Britain tomorrow
fuzzy logic 74

Gates, Bill 147
GE Capital 117
genetic algorithm 73-4
geographical information system (GIS) 96
Germany 23, 69, 82, 128
GLC 119
global health insurance scheme 69
Global Positioning System (GPS) satellites 149
global surveillance systems 39
global telephone tapping surveillance 39
globalisation, of trade 134
government 108-15
in the future 144-51
as a regulator 126-31
Government Electronic Mailbox 33
Government.Direct 38, 39
grand prix racing cars, smart management systems for 49-50
hackers and hacking 41, 124, 150, 152
HantsNet 22, 48, 92-3
HantsWeb 93
health care system, Europe-wide 69-70
health insurance scheme, global 69
health service, management 60-3
Healthpoint touch-screen kiosks 57
Helmsley, Leona 132-3
Heseltine, Michael 112
home shopping 148
hospitals without walls 61
hot desk systems 121

IBM 134
ICL 69, 71,93, 102, 104, 110, 112, 114
ICT 8, 12, 13, 24, 62, 63, 80, 111, 122, 127, 134, 137, 138, 146
India 86, 117
Indonesia 82
Infopolis 50
information kiosks, in hospitals 27
Information Revolution 13, 147, 148
Information Society Forum 25, 61
information warfare 149
infrastructure, electronic 104
Inland Revenue 99, 100, 135, 145
integrated electronic service centres 75
intelligent agents 8, 116
interactive community TV station (Berkeley, California) 75
interactive TV 17, 18, 29, 75
and consultations with patients 54
and health care professionals 58-9

157

Internet (the Net) 8
Intranet 8
Ionica 105
ISDN (integrated subscriber digital
 network) 56, 81, 104, 105, 118, 141
ISP 130, 131, 132

Japan 62
Johnstone, Sir Russell 20-1

Kamp, Karin 137, 138
kiosks 9, 14, 27, 75, 103-4

land and property information service 95
language, and future commercial relations
 118
learning 80-4, 114
learning-based education system 81
legal systems, in the future 31-2
libraries 75, 88-92
lifelong learning 80, 114
Local Government Association (LGA) 21
London Stock Exchange 41
London underground 45, 46

McKinsey 147
Malaysia 13, 82, 85, 115, 129, 130, 134,
 146, 147
Matrixx Marketing 119
medical records, on a microchip 62
medical staff, training of 59-60
microchip, medical records on a 62
microfiles 89
microfilms, of records 89-90
Microsoft 134
missiles, guided by satellites 149
MISTi kiosks 93
mobile phones 105
Mondex electronic purse 45
money laundering 41
money transfer 41, 42
motorways, digital cameras on 36
multimedia 9
multimedia kiosks 27, 101-2, 147
multipurpose smart cards 45
Munich police force 128
music-on-demand 90, 91

NASDAQ (North American Securities
 Dealers' Automated Quotations) 115
National Audit Office 123
National Health Service 60-1, 63
National Radiological Protection Board 105
National Sound Archive 94-5
NCR 102

neo-nazi material, on the Web 127
Netherlands, the 20
Nets 102
Netscape 134
network computers 9, 119
neural networking 73
New Zealand public sector reforms 113
Newham 27, 28
NewLink Project 83
NHS Executive 60
Norway 62
Norweb 106

OECD 137
off-planet commerce 132
on-line libraries 89
on-line services 137
One Stop Arts Shop 94
Open University 83
Oracle UK 85, 103
Organisation of Economic Co-operation
 Development 130
organised benefits fraud tracking 72
outsourcing 9, 121-3

Pacific Rim countries 13, 85, 144
Pakistan 86
pan-European library, for telemedicine 61
paramedics, US military 55-6
Parliamentary Web 23
patient, informing the 57-9
Patient Information Leaflets, on a
 CD-ROM database 57-8
pay-per-view 80
payment system, electronic 91
Periphera 83-4
Perot, Ross 29, 38, 122
personal identification numbers (PIN) 68
phantom identities 72
phone traffic, managing of incoming 119
pornography, on the Internet 127
Portugal 69
pregnant women, ultrasound tests for 54-5
price-per-transaction 122
private sector contractors 100, 101
Project Jukebox 95
Promise 50
Public Records Office 89
public sector, reducing overhead costs 123
pulse readers 68-9

QUBE system (Columbus, Ohio) 29

racist material, on the Web 127
radio-wave technologies 105

INDEX

radio-wave telephones, and brain tumours 105-6
reference libraries 89
improved access to existing records 90
Royal Bank of Scotland 110
rural areas 104-5, 141, 142, 148

satellite photographic surveillance 39
satellite and radio-wave technologies 105
Scandinavia 28
ScotLIS (Scotland's Royal Institute of Chartered Surveyors) 95
Scottish Office 95
Scottish Widows 121
security 92, 123-5
self-assessment 67
self-assessment forms, electronic 99
self-service society 66-76
sensors, for reading of fingerprints 68
Serbia 129
shared pool schemes 50
ShareLink 117
simulated road accidents 60
Singapore 13, 33-5, 38, 69, 85, 96-7, 102-3, 147
Sky TV 17, 18
smart cards 9, 45, 62, 67, 69, 91, 92, 146, 147
smart cards readers 27, 91
smart management systems, for grand prix racing cars 49-50
Social Security Administration (Fraud) Act (1997) 70, 71
Society of Information Technology Management 119
Soete, Luc 137, 138
South Africa 68, 105
South Korea 86
Spain 69
Statewatch 39-40
surveillance systems 128
swipe cards 69

tax, per parcel of information dispatched 136-7
tax evasion 135
taxation 133-6, 138, 139, 140
Taylor, Ian 17, 25, 103
telecommunications infrastructure 105, 141
teledemocracy 30
telematics 9
telemedicine 54-6, 145
telesurgery 54
telephone computer integration (TIC) 116
teleschooling 82

teleworking 83, 120-1
Texas, US 68
ticket selling, electronic 67
Time Warner 18
Titmuss Sainer Dechert 133
toll charging 48, 49
Touch Illinois 67
touch screen terminals 102
trade globalisation 134
traffic control, automatic distance 50
traffic crime, electronic recording of 36
transfer pricing 134
translators 28, 120
transport, in the future 43-51
travel revolution 44-51
TSNet 93

UK Citizens' Online Democracy 29
United States 23, 24, 25, 38, 54, 58, 62, 67, 68, 75, 82, 123-4, 135, 136
United States Immigration Auto-Clearance Service (Singapore) 34
United States' National Security Agency 149
US military paramedics 55-6
UUNet 139

video-conferencing 9, 34, 38
video-on-demand 18, 90, 91
video-telephony, for deaf people 83-4
virtual banks 148
virtual call centres 121
virtual campus 83
virtual classes 82
virtual libraries 88-92
virtual money 141
virtual reality, training surgeons through 59-60
viruses 150
voice activation systems 50
vouchers, electronic 81

wages, equalisation of 118
warfare, changing the nature of 149, 150
Web TV 18
welfare benefits fraud 71, 72
welfare rights databases 58
welfare state 64-76
wire transfers 131-2
Wirszycz, Rob 101
World Wide Web 9, 22, 23, 92-7, 116

year 2000 crisis 123